ROAD TO BERLIN

Below: Mulberry Harbours. Each harbour was as large as Gibraltar harbour, with iron breakwaters weighing 3,000 tons and vast concrete caissons, some of them 400ft in length. They were designed to land 12,000 tons of stores and 2,500 vehicles daily. Here, unloading is in full swing, opposite Omaha. (IWM - EA 41379)

ROAD TO BERLIN

The Allied Drive from Normandy

GEORGE FORTY

CASSELL

Cassell & Co
Wellington House, 125 Strand, London WC2R 0BB

British Library Cataloguing-in-Publication Data:
a catalogue record for this book is available from the
British Library

ISBN 0-304-35306-X

Distributed in the USA by Stirling Publishing Co. Inc.,
387 Park Avenue South, New York, NY 10016-8810.

Designed and edited by DAG Publications Ltd.
Designed by David Gibbons; layout by Anthony A. Evans;
edited by Michael Boxall; printed and bound in Great
Britain.

ACKNOWLEDGEMENTS
I must thank the following photographic sources for
allowing me to use their evocative images: The Imperial
War Museum; the Tank Museum; the National Archives of
Canada; the National Archives of America; the US Army
and US Signal Corps; Real War Photos, Indiana; the Patton
Museum of Cavalry and Armor; Mr Bruce Robertson and
other individual sources as shown in the photographic
credits.

Contents

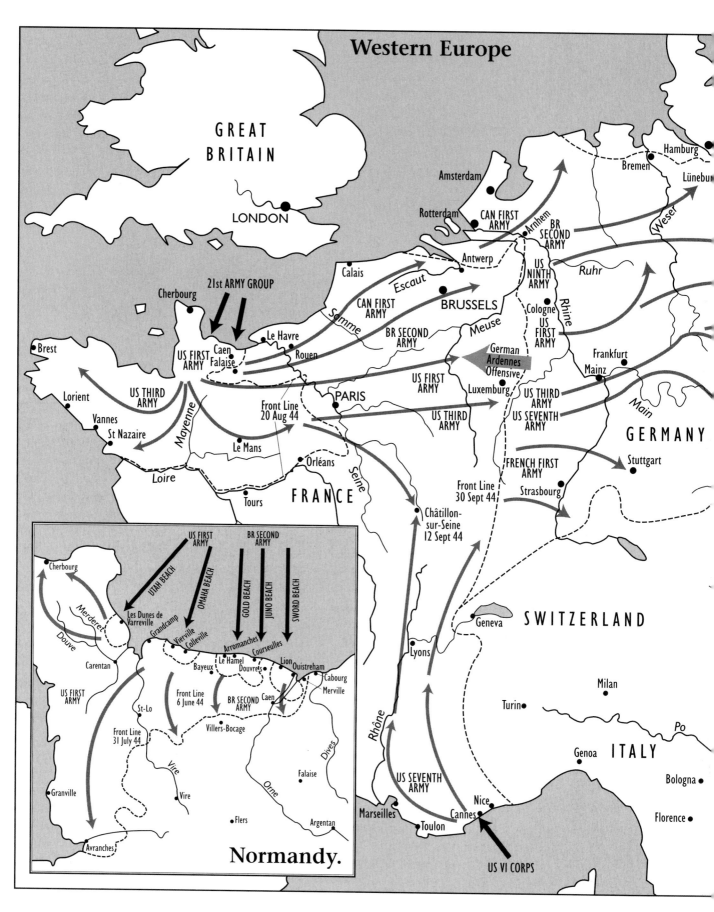

Western Europe

GREAT BRITAIN

LONDON

Cherbourg

21st ARMY GROUP

US FIRST ARMY

Caen
Falaise

Le Havre

Rouen

Brest

US THIRD ARMY

Lorient

Vannes

St Nazaire

Mayenne

Le Mans

Front Line
20 Aug 44

PARIS

Orléans

Loire

FRANCE

Tours

Seine

Calais

Escaut

Somme

CAN FIRST ARMY

BR SECOND ARMY

BRUSSELS

US FIRST ARMY

US THIRD ARMY

Amsterdam

Rotterdam

Antwerp

CAN FIRST ARMY

BR SECOND ARMY

Meuse

German
Ardennes
Offensive

Luxemburg

Châtillon-
sur-Seine
12 Sept 44

Arnhem

BR SECOND ARMY

US NINTH ARMY

Cologne

US FIRST ARMY

US THIRD ARMY

US SEVENTH ARMY

FRENCH FIRST ARMY

Front Line
30 Sept 44

Strasbourg

Hamburg

Bremen

Lüneburg

Weser

Ruhr

Rhine

Frankfurt

Mainz

Main

GERMANY

Stuttgart

SWITZERLAND

Geneva

Lyons

Rhône

Marseilles

Toulon

US SEVENTH ARMY

Cannes

Nice

US VI CORPS

Milan

Turin

Genoa

ITALY

Bologna

Florence

Po

Normandy.

US FIRST ARMY

BR SECOND ARMY

Cherbourg

Merderet

Douve

UTAH BEACH

OMAHA BEACH

GOLD BEACH

JUNO BEACH

SWORD BEACH

Les Dunes de
Varreville

Grandcamp

Vierville
Colleville

Arromanches

Courseulles

Le Hamel

Douvrets

Lion

Ouistreham

Cabourg

Merville

Carentan

Bayeux

Caen

US FIRST ARMY

St-Lo

Front Line
6 June 44

BR SECOND ARMY

Villers-Bocage

Front Line
31 July 44

Dives

Vire

Orne

Falaise

Granville

Vire

Flers

Argentan

Avranches

Introduction

Even a brief glance at this book will quickly show that it is short on text and long on visual images and this is in line with its main purpose, namely to tell by photographs the story of the Allied campaign in North West Europe, in the twelve months, June 1944 to May 1945. However, despite the fact that there are more than 280 photographs and one map, it was clearly impossible for me to cover every noteworthy event, every important action, every main town or city liberated, every enemy stronghold captured, every enemy army defeated and thus to tell the complete story of every one of the five million plus men who fought in the campaigns. 'Why didn't you include ...?' is bound to be the comment from some readers, but I hope that I have done enough to satisfy the majority.

In his incomparable history of the Second World War, Churchill says that the invasion of Europe was what the Western Powers might justly regard as being, 'the supreme climax of the war', and goes on to aver that although the road might be long and hard, never: '... could we doubt that decisive victory would be gained'.

In his autobiography of the war years, General Dwight D. Eisenhower, the Supreme Allied Expeditionary Force Commander, sets out in a chapter concerned with the planning of 'Overlord', the outline of the proposed Allied operations. I would summarise his words as follows:

1. To land on the coast of Normandy.
2. To build up the necessary resources to fight and win the decisive battle in the Normandy–Brittany region.
3. To break out from encircling enemy positions and pursue the enemy on a broad front with two Army Groups. The left-flank Army Group would have the major tasks of securing ports so as to ensure maintenance of supplies, and then, on reaching the boundaries of Germany, of threatening the Ruhr. The right-flank Army Group would advance in step, linking up with the forces that it was intended would invade southern France, then together they would advance eastwards.
4. To build up forces and supplies along the western borders of Germany, securing ports in Belgium and Brittany to facilitate this build-up.
5. While the build-up was taking place, to maintain an unrelenting offensive, so as to wear down the enemy and thus gain advantages for the final battles.
6. To complete the destruction of enemy forces west of the Rhine, while constantly seeking opportunities to seize bridge-heads across the river.
7. Having crossed the Rhine in strength, to launch a final offensive in a double envelopment of the Ruhr, emphasising the left prong, and following this up with an immediate thrust through Germany (the specific direction of this final thrust to be determined at the time).
8. Finally, to clean out the rest of 'Greater Germany', linking up with Soviet forces advancing from the east.

In his book Eisenhower states that: 'This general plan, carefully outlined at staff meetings before D-Day, was never abandoned, even momentarily, throughout the campaign.' In general terms this is true, except of course for one digression when the unexpected German offensive in the Ardennes had to be dealt with.

This then is what I have used as the basic structure of *Road to Berlin*, and I hope it will provide the reader with an interesting and illuminating record of what was one of the great moments in the history of man, certainly in the 20th century and possibly of all time.

George Forty
Bryantspuddle, Dorset
September 1998

7

1
That First Toehold

Although this book is primarily about the progress of the Allied armies across North West Europe from Normandy to Berlin, a short description of the monumental event which preceded the mobile battles is essential. This of course was the Allied landings on the coast of Normandy which took place on D-Day, 6 June 1944.

A Second Front

Virtually from the time when Hitler launched his invasion of Russia, the Soviets had been continually pressing first the British then the Americans and British, to open up a 'Second Front', to take pressure off the USSR. However, firm agreement as to a suitable date for this momentous undertaking did not come until the Trident Conference, held in Washington 11–25 May 1943, when Churchill and Roosevelt and their advisers agreed that May 1944 would be the earliest feasible date for such an invasion to be launched. This was then changed to early June, the chosen day being the 5th, in turn postponed for 24 hours because of bad weather.

Although the Allies had already planned the invasion of Sicily (10 July 1943), to be followed by that of Italy (3 and 9 September 1943), and despite Churchill's misgivings that any invasion of northern France might well turn into a blood bath, it was decided to land there, with just the short 'hop' across the English Channel, rather than to reinforce success in the Mediterranean. It has also to be said that the Americans, suspecting Churchill of 'Balkan intrigues', scotched any effort proposed there. After much deliberation the Normandy beaches between Cherbourg and Le Havre were chosen, despite the very tempting and much shorter approach offered by the Pas-de-Calais. Normandy did offer many advantages – the beaches and inland terrain were

suitable, the area was in easy reach from RAF and USAAF bases in southern England, the distance by sea was reasonable and, because the Germans were convinced that the blow would fall in the Pas-de-Calais, the Atlantic Wall defences were not as strong there. Indeed, having made their decision to go for Normandy, the Allies, by means of an elaborate and many-faceted cover plan (Operation 'Fortitude'), did their very best to ensure that the Germans continued to expect the major landing to be in the Pas-de-Calais. Fortunately, this cover plan worked brilliantly.

One major drawback to the chosen area was the absence of any immediate port facilities. This was compensated by the two amazing prefabricated 'Mulberry' harbours; these were in effect enormous hollow concrete caissons that would be towed across the Channel and sunk off two of the selected invasion beaches to form breakwaters. Nearly all the UK's concrete production had gone into making these caissons, and in addition, a number of old warships and merchantmen had been earmarked for use as outer breakwaters.[1] Another revolutionary means of supply was PLUTO – the Pipeline Under The Ocean – which would enable fuel to be pumped from England to France, forming a lifeline to the Allied forces on the continent.

By the early spring of 1944, the Allies had built up a massive army in the United Kingdom, comprising many thousands of American, British, Canadian and other Allied troops, with an enormous array of up-to-date weapons, vehicles and equipment, backed by a vast number of naval and air force units, with an estimated total strength of more than three million men. For Operation 'Overlord' overall operational command of Allied ground forces would be vested in General Sir Bernard Montgomery's HQ 21st Army Group, with troops

Above: Well laden British paratroopers board their aircraft on the night 5/6 June 1944. They and their American counterparts will be the first Allied troops to land in France. (IWM - CH 13303)

from US First Army and British Second Army (the latter containing both British and Canadian troops). They were of course under the overall command of General Dwight D. Eisenhower, Supreme Commander Allied Expeditionary Force, and his SHAEF headquarters. The sea landings would be made on five carefully selected beaches, code-named (from west to east): 'Utah', 'Omaha', 'Gold', 'Juno', 'Sword' and would be preceded by an airborne assault at 0200 hrs (some 4½ hours before the first seaborne waves hit the beaches) by American and British airborne forces. Massive air strikes by some 2,500 bombers and 7,000 fighter-bombers would soften up the beach-head areas – not forgetting to bomb the rest of the coast, especially in the Pas-de-Calais in order to maintain the illusion that anything happening in the Normandy area was merely a feint attack. The numbing effect of the mass bombing would be thickened up by shore bombardment from 700 warships – including five battleships, 23 cruisers and more than 100 destroyers, which were to escort the landing forces. Backing up all this activity would be a much longer bombing campaign, spread over some 3–4 weeks prior to D-Day and covering the coastal area in depth, aiming at disrupting all road and rail communications, so as to make it as difficult as possible for the enemy to bring up reinforcements.

On the other side of the Channel, the German defenders were dogged by both indecision and over-confidence. Field Marshal Erwin Rommel, hero of North Africa and now commander of Army Group B, some of whose troops had direct responsibility for the Normandy beaches, appreciated more than anyone how weak the 'Atlantic Wall' really was. He had been trying hard to get Hitler to visit the area, so that he could explain the situation, make him realise how short his Army Group was of both manpower and *matériel*, and impress upon his Führer the vital necessity to be able to control the deployment of the all-important armoured reserve, which Rommel needed as close to the coast as possible because he wanted to fight his main battle on the beaches before the enemy had time to get a foothold. When it became clear that Hitler

Above: Camouflaged with blackened faces, the paratroopers take up their positions in the aircraft. (IWM - CH 13304)

Below: RAF Tarrant Rushton, Dorset. On the runway are the Halifax tugs and Horsa/Hamilcar gliders for the second lift on D-Day. This photograph was taken from the aerodrome's Tiger Moth at around 1800hrs on D-Day, the aircraft being part of Operation 'Mallard', when 32 Halifax, towing 30 Hamilcars and 2 Horsas, took off between 1928 and 1959hrs. Only one Halifax was lost. (Bruce Roberston)

would never come to France, Rommel decided to go to see him instead and arranged for a personal interview on 6 June. It had been decided that the Allies would be unlikely to invade during the period 5–8 June because of unfavourable tides; moreover none of the Luftwaffe's recent reconnaissance reports had indicated any obvious pre-invasion activity. Few among the German High Command appreciated the fact that once the invasion was under way, overwhelming Allied air superiority would make German troop movement so difficult as to be virtually impossible. Those whose experience had been on the Eastern Front, where the Luftwaffe had generally more than held its own, just did not believe the picture painted for them by Rommel who had had to suffer the problem in North Africa.

Determined to win the Führer over to his way of thinking, Rommel set off, intending to go to Berchtesgarten via his home in Herrlingen because his wife Lucie's birthday was on 6 June. Air travel had been banned for senior officers, because of the threat from Allied air activity, so he left by car on the 5th and was at home on the fateful night 5/6 June. The general consensus among the German High Command was that, while it was agreed that the Allies would attempt a landing within the next few weeks, the defences would be sufficient to deal with such landings, the Pas-de-Calais still being the most favoured site for such an attempt. Rommel arrived home safely and was rung up by his chief of staff (Speidel) between 0600–0630 hrs who told him about the landings and the action Army Group B had taken. He immediately cancelled his visit to Hitler and returned posthaste to his headquarters, arriving at La Roche Guyon by 2000 hrs that evening.

Airborne landings. Between midnight and 0200 hrs American and British airborne forces were dropped or air-landed on their target areas. These were to secure the flanks of the beach-head area, destroy vital bridges, gun positions, etc. In the west, US 101st Airborne Division (Ab Div) had the job of taking and holding the causeways which formed the exits from Utah Beach, across the marshy ground just inland. The US 82nd Ab Div were to be

Top left: Men of 508th Regt, US 82nd Ab Div, make a last-minute check of their equipment before taking off from an airfield in Saltby, England on 6 June 1944. (US Army via Real War Photos - AB 2022)

Lower left: British Horsa gliders scattered over their landing zone near Caen. (Bruce Robertson)

Above: Four members of the US 82nd Ab Div enter the village of Ste-Mère-Eglise under heavy enemy artillery fire on 6 June 1944. (US Army via Real War Photos - AB 2023)

Below: Weymouth, Dorset, American Rangers visit a temporary 'doughnut dugout' for a cup of coffee and a doughnut, provided as always by the American Red Cross, before boarding HMS *Prins Leopold*, to assault Point du Hoc. (US National Archives)

landed farther inland to clear the area between Ste-Mère-Eglise and Pont-l'Abbé, but the inexperience of many of the pilots meant that both divisions' drops were widely scattered with the result that the paratroops were very thin on the ground. Nevertheless they fought hard and bravely and had a certain amount of luck – for example, they attacked the HQ of German 91st Air Landing Division and killed the commander, Lieutenant-General Wilhelm Falley, the first German general to be killed during the invasion, thus leaving his division leaderless. On the eastern flank, the British 6th Ab Div had three main tasks: to take and hold various crossings over the River Orne and the Caen Canal between Caen and Ouistreham; to storm the Merville battery; to blow up various bridges over the River Dives. Despite some of the troops being landed in the wrong locations, all these tasks were achieved and the positions were held until relieved from the beaches.

Seaborne landings. The Allied 21st Army Group (see Annex 'A' for outline organisation)

were to land on the five beach areas as detailed below, close armoured support being provided by amphibious DD tanks and other remarkable armoured fighting vehicles from British 79th Armoured Division (the 'Funnies'). These included mine-clearing vehicles, bridgelayers, flame-throwers, engineer vehicles and many others. They would prove to be exceptionally useful. Allied naval forces were commanded by Admiral Sir Bertram Ramsay and air forces by Air Chief Marshal Sir Trafford Leigh-Mallory. D-Day was originally scheduled for Monday, 5 June 1944, but rough seas and high winds brought a delay of 24 hours.

Utah Beach. Situated on the east coast of the Cotentin peninsula at les Dunes-de-Varreville, this was General J. Lawton Collins' US VII Corps' objective. At 0630 hrs, led by US 4th Infantry Division, they landed on the southern sector of the beach with little resistance, but marshy ground delayed their advance inland. Some 28 of their 32 amphibious DD tanks reached the beach fifteen minutes after the leading wave, so were able to give close supporting fire. By the end of the day more than 23,000 men had been landed, they had achieved their set D-Day objectives, and fewer than 250 had been killed or wounded.

Omaha Beach. Some eight miles east of Utah, General Leonard Gerow's US V Corps landed here, led by US 1st Infantry Division ('The Big Red One'). They were in trouble from the outset. Because of the exceedingly rough sea, the infantry, engineers and artillery were transhipped into landing-craft too far out, and many of the amphibious tanks were launched too early and sank before they could make the beach. Visibility was poor and as a result most of the bombing was too far inland and the naval covering fire fell too short. Enemy return fire was both heavy and accurate. The density of underwater obstacles was considerable and the enemy had recently been reinforced. The initial assault was held at the edge of the water, subsequent waves making only slow and painful progress. Towards mid-morning the tide of battle began to change; large landing-

Left: Royal Marine Commandos making their way ashore at St-Aubin-sur-Mer. The small motor cycle being manhandled over the waves belonged to 4th SS Bde HQ. (IWM - B 5218)

Left: Commandos on the beach. The landing at St-Aubin was directly under heavy enemy fire and No 48 Commando suffered many casualties before they could move inland. (IWM - MH 33543)

Left: An LCT about to ground on Red Beach (Sword Area). The time is about 35 minutes after H hour ' Note the column of AFVS belonging to 27th Armd Bde also landing – the leading tank near the two houses appears to be on fire. (IWM - B 5111)

Above: This splendid photograph was taken on the afternoon of D-Day as the Stormont, Dundas and Glengarry Highlanders of Canadian 9th Brigade came ashore on White Beach, Nan Sector (Juno area) at Bernières-sur-Mer. (Public Archives Canada - PA 122765)

craft, despite the obstacles, forced their way to the beach, and destroyers risked running aground to get closer and engage their targets more accurately. By nightfall some 34,000 men had been landed, but more than 1,000 GIs had been killed and many more wounded; they had not achieved their first objectives and were still less than a mile inland. But they were holding the villages of Vierville-sur-Mer, St-Laurent and Colleville-sur-Mer, which controlled the east–west road, and were determined to resist all counter-attacks. To the west of Omaha, 2nd Ranger Battalion had landed three companies at the foot of the cliffs at Pointe du Hoc, where the Germans had coastal defence artillery positions. After fierce fighting they managed to destroy the guns, and hold the position against heavy counter-attacks.

Gold Beach. Some ten miles east of Omaha. General G. C. Bucknall's British XXX Corps, led by 50th Infantry Division and 8th Armoured Brigade, landed here. Because of the tides, the landings here and farther east were later than those on the two US beaches so there was no surprise. Bad weather, fierce currents and high winds, hampered the approach, so the landing-craft carrying the DD tanks were brought right up on to the beach rather than run the risk of being swamped in the heavy surf. The initial advance inland was fairly rapid, but the D-Day objectives of

Bayeux and the main road to Caen were not reached. By nightfall the 'toehold' was some five square miles in area, reserves were ashore and aggressive patrolling was nearing Bayeux. Some 25,000 men had been landed at a cost of 500 dead.

Juno Beach. About 5 miles east of Gold. This was allocated to General John Crocker's British I Corps whose Canadian 3rd Infantry Division supported by Canadian 2nd Armoured Brigade led the way. The beach area was wide enough to land two brigades side by side. Some of the underwater obstacles were especially troublesome, but the amphibious DD tanks were launched successfully only 100 yards or so from shore and were thus available to support the infantry, effectively silencing the enemy strongpoints. Some 21,500 men got ashore and pushed inland towards Bretteville and Caen, but were held up by enemy pressure and the inevitable traffic jams. By nightfall their progress was roughly level with the left flank of Gold's troops, but there was still a 2-mile gap between them and Sword Beach's troops to their left. They were also a few miles short of their original objectives, but were in a strong position from which they were determined not to be moved.

Sword Beach. About 5 miles east of Juno. More elements of Crocker's British I Corps landed here, led by 3rd Infantry Division,

Above: A tank of the Canadian Ist Hussars, from London, Ontario, coming ashore on the afternoon of D-Day. Note also the Royal Canadian Engineers busy trying to make the beach passable with the aid of an armoured bulldozer. Getting off the beach quickly was extremely difficult but it was essential if the beach-head was to be protected from counter-attacks. (Public Archives Canada - PA 128791)

Below: Maj Gen Rod Keller commanding 3rd Canadian Division is seen here on the afternoon of D-Day, impressing on his troops that they must be ready for the inevitable German counter-attack. Keller was one of the best Canadian operational commanders, hence his being the choice for this vital role on D-Day. (Public Archives Canada - PA 115544)

Above: A group of wounded Canadian soldiers wait to be transferred to a Casualty Clearing Station on D + 1. On the whole, casualties were light, considering the scale of the operation. (Canadian Offical Photograph - 33757-N)

Below: An appropriately-named AVRE of 77 Assault Sqn RE is parked in Lion-sur-Mer, whilst the carriers passing by belong to the 2nd Bn, The Middlesex Regiment – a machine gun battalion. The AVRE was based upon the Churchill tank and mounted a 290mm spigot mortar, called a Petard, as its main armament, for use against enemy blockhouses, etc. (IWM - B 5040)

supported by 27th Armoured Brigade, together with several Commando and Marine units who immediately pressed inland to link up and relieve the paratroops. As with Juno, there was congestion, but they managed to reach Biéville and to beat off a counter-attack from 21st Panzer Division. By nightfall nearly 29,000 troops were ashore and, although the original first day objectives were not reached, the Orne bridges had been seized.

Summary. Undoubtedly Operation 'Overlord' had been a success. Some 155,000 troops were now ashore and, with the protection afforded by continuous naval and air operations, they were there to stay. Omaha had been the most difficult beach to secure and the US 1st Inf Div in particular had suffered many casualties. They had not all reached their D-Day objectives, but were firmly established everywhere. In the British/Canadian sector, the leading troops were now off the beaches, the front line was, on average, some six miles inland and they had withstood a heavy counter-attack from 21st Pz Div. Despite the fact that the inland penetration was only half that hoped for, the chances of the enemy pushing them quickly off the beach-head were now remote. In addition, the casualties had been much lighter than expected. The remarkable British 'Funnies' of 79th Armd Div had more than proved their worth. Now it was vital to link up the beach-heads, get more troops, their weapons and equipment ashore and start to push inland. 'We had achieved surprise,' Montgomery wrote. 'The troops had fought magnificently and our losses had been much lower than had ever seemed possible. We had breached the Atlantic Wall along the whole Neptune frontage and all assaulting divisions were ashore. To sum up, the results of D-Day were extremely encouraging, although the weather remained a great anxiety.'[2]

Notes

1. Parts of the Mulberry harbours can still be seen off the Normandy coast; two of the caissons were later brought back to Portland, Dorset, where they remain.
2. Montgomery, B. *Normandy to the Baltic.*

THAT FIRST TOEHOLD

Left: Tank crews snatch a few minutes rest whilst they and their Sherman tanks and Bren carriers wait to advance. Lion-sur-Mer, 6 June 1944. (IWM - B 5033)

Below: On the day after D-Day (7 June), a tracked Bofors LAA gun awaits the Luftwaffe, next to a disabled Sherman DD tank on the Canadian beach. The Bofors is mounted on a British Crusader III AA Mk I chassis – note the all-round open-topped shield. The 'Duplex-Drive' Sherman has its flotation screen lowered. (Public Archives Canada - PA 132897)

Organization of 21st Army Group for Operation 'Overlord' (initial phase)

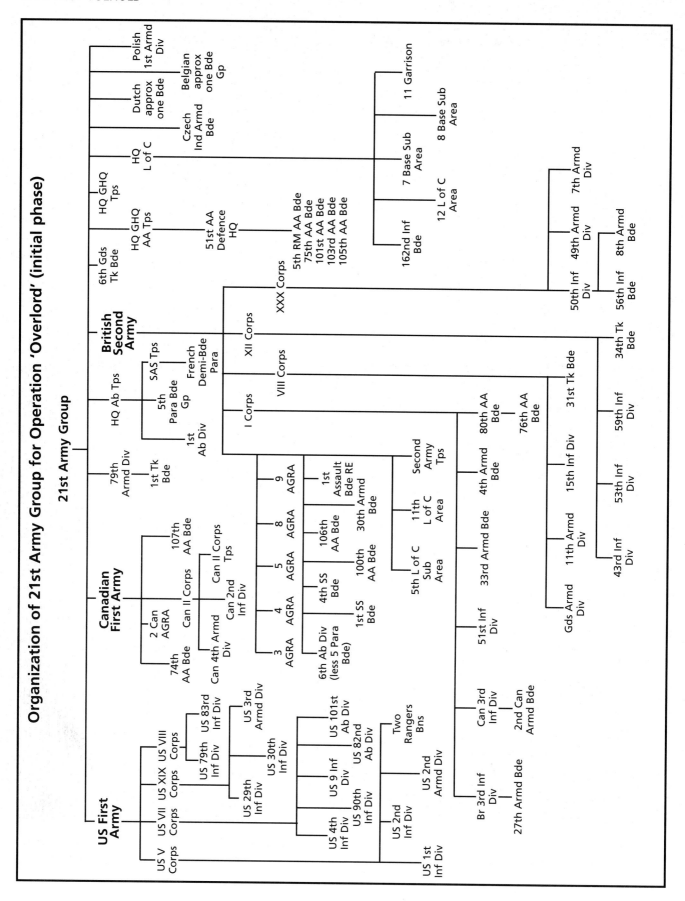

Above: 105mm M7 Priest self-propelled guns in action by the side of a field in Lion-sur-Mer. The M7 and M7B1 Howitzer Motor Carriage mounted a 105mm howitzer on the M3 and M4 medium tank chassis. They were the standard equipment in all American armoured divisions as well as in many Allied ones. (IWM - B 5032)

2
Building-up the Beach-head

Rommel Thwarted
Now that the first toehold had been achieved it was necessary to secure and expand the beach-head before the defenders could launch a size-able counter-stroke. For a variety of reasons

Rommel was prevented from mounting any major counter-attacks, foremost among which being the Allies' total air supremacy over the battlefield area which prompted Rommel to make a formal complaint to the Luftwaffe for

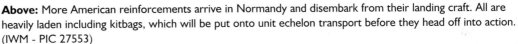

Above: More American reinforcements arrive in Normandy and disembark from their landing craft. All are heavily laden including kitbags, which will be put onto unit echelon transport before they head off into action. (IWM - PIC 27553)

Left: D + I and more reinforcements arrive. Men of the 2nd Infantry Division, US Army, climb up the sand dunes off Easy Red sector, Omaha Beach, past a captured German bunker on their way to face enemy fire for the very first time. (Bruce Robertson)

the total lack of support his hard-pressed troops were receiving. For example, on 7 June when I SS Panzer Corps were trying to assemble for the first major counter-stroke against the landings, they were severely harassed, delayed and disorganised by continual air attacks until 9 June, by which time the Allies' reinforcement had been such that a 'sweeping the invaders into the sea' move by the panzers, was out of the question. Furthermore the unremitting Allied bombing of road and rail communications, especially in northern France, was so successful that the movement of reinforcements was virtually impossible, especially by day. These difficulties were compounded by

the stepping-up of subversive operations by the French *Maquis*. Thousands of these resistance fighters were in the area, many of them armed to the teeth, ready to assist the invaders with acts of sabotage, which severely disrupted the rail network. Worst of all, there was continual interference with Rommel's planning from the very top – namely, from Adolf Hitler – who, still convinced that the Allied landings were a feint and that the real invasion would come in the Pas-de-Calais, refused to allow Rommel free rein over the reserves, in particular, the vital Panzer Group West.

Despite the enemy's problems, the consolidation of the beach-heads was still not easy.

Above: Another unloading scene, this time on one of the British beaches. Note the 40mm Bofors Light AA gun in position to provide additional AA cover. The Swedish-designed gun was built under licence in both UK and USA. It was undoubtedly the best LAA gun of the war. (IWM - HU 3022)

Below: US Army vehicles leaving the beach, led by a heavily laden M3 half-track. The ubiquitous half-track was used for many jobs, eg: as a weapons platform for a wide variety of AA, anti-tank, small artillery pieces, mortars, etc, also for personnel as seen here and as a battlefield stores carrier. (IWM - MH 25279)

Once the individual beaches had been linked up it was vital to secure a proper working harbour – the obvious one being Cherbourg. This necessitated clearing the Cotentin peninsula and cutting it off from the rest of Normandy. At the same time, the Mulberry harbours had to be established off Omaha and Gold Beaches, a 'belt and braces' move which would prove doubly fortuitous because Cherbourg harbour when finally captured was found to be completely wrecked. 'I ordered the armies to proceed with the plan,' wrote Montgomery later. 'United States First Army was to complete the capture of its D-Day objectives, secure Carentan and Isigny so as to link up its beach-heads, and then thrust across the base of the peninsula to isolate Cherbourg as a prelude to its reduction. British Second Army was to continue the battle for Caen, develop the bridge-head southwards across the Bayeux–Caen road and link up with United States V Corps at Port-en-Bessin.'[1]

Week 1: 7–12 June 1944[2]

Wednesday 7 June. In the west, US forces on Utah began to link up with the paratroops and move inland towards Montebourg in the north and Carentan in the south, while those from Omaha pushed towards Isigny and Bayeux, reaching Formigny. General Eisenhower visited the front that day and ordered V and VII Corps to link up as soon as they had taken Carentan (101st Ab Div) and Isigny (29th Inf Div). In the far north 4th Inf Div advanced towards the line Quinéville (on the coast) to Montebourg, but was held up by a line of German fortifications in the Crisbecq–Azeville area, while 8 RCT went to the

Below: Commandos near Caen. Commando troops resting in a narrow lane near Caen on 7 June, after taking part in some very heavy fighting. (IWM - B 5077)

support of 82nd Ab Div which was facing a dangerous counter-attack in the Ste-Mère-Eglise area and at the La Fière bridge across the River Merderet. South of Ste-Mère-Eglise paratroopers of 101st Ab Div established a bridgehead across the River Douve, capturing the garrisons of Le Port and La Barquette. Progress out of Omaha was slower, and although both 29th and 1st Divs pressed forward towards Isigny and Bayeux, they had mixed success – the enemy held Formigny on the right, but the Americans captured Huppain on the left. The Germans managed to maintain a corridor astride the River Drôme, between the US and British/Canadian forces, up to its confluence with the River Aure. Reinforcements including US 2nd Inf Div came ashore that evening.

In British Second Army's sector, 50th Inf Div captured Bayeux and pushed units down to the Bayeux–Caen road, as did Can 3rd Inf Div in the east, near Caen.

Thursday 8 June. The Allied second wave was now almost completely ashore and US 4th Inf Div (VII Corps) plus units of 82nd Ab Div began to push towards the port of Cherbourg, but were again held up by the fortifications in the Crisbecq–Azeville area. Fierce fighting followed, while units of US V Corps took Isgny, but failed to link up with VII Corps who were fighting for Carentan. Further east, Tour-en-Bessin and Ste-Anne were taken, but the enemy could not be cut off as he evacuated Port-en-Bessin. Nevertheless 47th Regt RM entered the village in the early hours of the morning and the link between Omaha and Gold was achieved.

Friday 9 June. US 4th Inf Div made a major breakthrough in its advance towards Cherbourg when they broke through the Azeville fortifications (found to be massive reinforced casemates disguised as ordinary houses, linked by trenches with overhead cover and

Below: It is 9 June and these GIs are sheltering from heavy enemy shell-fire on Omaha, which hindered unloading until the batteries at St Marcouf and Azeville could be captured. (IWM - EA 25902)

containing 150mm guns and many machine-guns). Quinéville was the next objective. In the centre of the peninsula, 82nd Ab Div attacked towards the River Merderet, while 101st Ab went for Carentan again. In V Corps' area, 2nd Inf Div troops entered Trévières and pushed on towards Rubercy; in the east US 1st Inf Div reached Agy and Dodigny. US 2nd Armd Div began to land. British and Canadian forces were in action against increasing enemy reserves around Caen. Allied aircraft were now operating from strips in Normandy. It is also relevant to note that on the Italian Front certain US troops, mostly from VI Corps, were pulled out of action in preparation for the coming invasion of southern France (see later). **Saturday 10 June.** US 9th Inf Div came ashore and by the end of the day the Allies had some 325,000 men in the beach-head. The link-up between Utah and Omaha beaches was at last achieved, thanks to an advance by 2nd Armd

Div, but the Germans were still holding Carentan despite 101st Ab Div's efforts to surround the town. In V Corps' area US 1st Inf Div reached the Bayeux–St-Lô road. In British Second Army's sector the first major offensive (Operation 'Perch') was launched; the intention being to make a wide outflanking manoeuvre west of Caen, cross the River Odon and take the high ground around Evrecy. The attack made little progress, mainly because the opposition consisted of the crack *Panzer Lehr* Division and the equally formidable 12th SS Panzer Division around Tilly-sur-Seules. This village changed hands twice, the British eventually being driven out by a fierce counter-attack. East of Caen the opposition facing I Corps was equally strong, elements of German LXXXVI Corps bringing the advance to a halt. General Montgomery established his HQ in France that day. As more panzers came into action, the superiority of the Tiger's 8.8cm gun

Below: Link-up. Men of the British 12th Para Bn enjoy a cuppa, having linked up with the main ground forces on 10 June, after fighting virtually a guerrilla war behind enemy lines. (IWM - B 5349)

and the Panther's long-barrelled 7.5cm gun became more and more apparent, especially as the close bocage countryside favoured the defence.[3]

Sunday 11 June. Units of US 90th Inf Div continued their advance west of the Merderet, while 101st Ab put in a fierce attack on Carentan which the Germans evacuated during the night to escape the heavy American artillery fire. The GIs occupied the town, but in the morning they came under heavy enemy pressure to re-occupy it. In the British sector, British armour encountered heavy resistance around Tilly-sur-Seulles. They took the village but were counter-attacked and forced out. Farther east, resistance was equally strong around Caen.

Monday 12 June. Although US VII Corps had still not completely reached its D-Day objectives, they were still advancing up the Cotentin peninsula towards Cherbourg and southwards towards St-Lô. On the eastern coast of the peninsula first Crisbecq then Azeville were taken, but Montebourg remained in enemy hands. Other VII Corps units were fighting their way westwards across the peninsula and south-westwards from Carentan. V Corps was supporting them and, on its left flank, 1st Inf Div were advancing towards the St-Lô–Caen road, taking Caumont. By the end of the first week some 326,000 men were ashore, together with 104,000 tons of supplies and 54,000 vehicles.

Above: Mulberry Harbours. Two prefabricated harbours were towed across the Channel and constructed. Mulberry 'A' – seen here – was opposite Omaha and although not scheduled to be fully operational until D + 18 (24 June), it was in use earlier. The photograph shows one of the two Loebnitz pierheads. (Bruce Robertson)

Summary. It can be fairly stated that by the end of the first week all four Allied Corps which had taken part in the assault were firmly ashore, had joined up all five beach-heads and linked up with the airborne forces. They had thus established a sizeable lodgement area with a continuous perimeter within which were secure logistic areas. The entire beach-head was under the protection of an almost impenetrable air and sea 'umbrella'. All that was lacking was port facilities and these would soon be available as the various components of the Mulberry Harbours were brought

across. Assembly, however, took longer than anticipated and neither Mulberry was anywhere near completion by the end of the first week.

Week 2: 13–19 June 1944

The second week began with an embarrassing reverse for one of the most renowned British armoured divisions – 7th Armd Div (The Desert Rats) – which had been switched to the right of XXX Corps and was advancing swiftly southwards, taking Villers-Bocage. On quitting the village, however, the division's 22nd Armd Bde encountered panzer ace Obersturmführer Michael Wittmann and his four Tiger tanks, who knocked out almost the entire divisional advance guard, destroying 23 tanks and numerous other vehicles and bringing the advance to a shuddering halt. Elsewhere 17th Pz Div almost succeeded in retaking Carentan, so pressure to restrict the enlargement of the beach-head was considerable. However, on the 14th US XIX Corps became

Below: Gooseberry Shelters. The first and simplest form of breakwater to protect the invasion beaches from rough seas, were blockships – known as the 'Corncob Fleet', which were deliberately sunk. For example, there were 59 elderly merchantmen and warships, which sailed down from Scotland to Poole harbour prior to D-Day, ready for their final journey to Normandy, where they were sunk. Behind this line of blockships can be seen a Whale Pierhead. (IWM - C4846)

operational in the area between US V and VII Corps, and next day US VIII Corps also became operational. By the end of Week 2, US forces had pushed forward up the Cotentin peninsula to the general line Quinéville–Valognes–Les Pieux. Trapped German troops were refused permission to attempt to breakout – in fact Hitler refused to allow any withdrawals from any area. From Omaha, US V and XIX Corps had pushed forward to Caumont, but movement was still difficult in the British/Canadian area. At a meeting with Rommel and von Rundstedt (overall commander in the west) at Soissons on 17 June, Hitler raged at them, accusing them and all their troops of cowardice. The Allies were also having their share of misfortunes. After assembling the two Mulberry harbours and getting them close to readiness, hours of labour were brought to nought by severe gales, which would last until the 22nd,

irreparably damaging Mulberry A (off Omaha) and severely damaging Mulberry B (at Arromanches). The Mulberries had been expected to handle some 15,000 tons of cargo daily, rising to 46,000 tons by D+90, so the damage was very worrying.

Week 3: 20–26 June 1944

By 20 June, American troops were only some five miles from Cherbourg and by the end of the week after hard fighting by the three attacking divisions against fanatical opposition, and accompanied by more than 1,000 tons of bombs, plus gunfire from the battleship HMS *Rodney*, the monitor HMS *Roberts* and other naval vessels, the port was almost entirely in their hands, apart from the actual dock area which was ruined. The German naval commander, Admiral Hennecke, and the garrison commander, General von Schlieben, were both captured on the 26th. Off the

Below: Mulberry Harbours. No one could have anticipated the ferocity of the great storm which began at 0330hrs 19 June and blew for three days and three nights – the worst summer gale for 80 years. The photograph shows the storm-twisted piers of the wrecked Omaha Mulberry. Eventually, enough was salvaged to restore Mulberry 'B' off the British beaches at Arromanches. (US Army - SC 198165)

Above: At low tide some vessels - like the Norwegian SS *Vestmanrad* seen here, were beached, so that unloading into DUKWs/trucks was made much easier. (Bruce Robertson)

Below: Scene at the Regimental Aid Post of 6 DLI, 50th Inf Div, after the battle of Lingevres, showing both British and German casualties being treated, 14 June 1944. (IWM - B 55270)

Left: Prisoners taken by American troops in the close bocage country are quizzed by an officer before being sent to the rear. One has been bandaged for a head wound. (IWM - AP 28446)

Below: This hut has been turned into a regimental aid post for American casualties near Mortain, south of Vire in Normandy. (IWM - EA 33190)

Right: American soldiers break through a smoke-screen to surround a wrecked building in the village Sainteny in western Normandy. (IWM - KY 30309)

Below: This young GI is trying to draw enemy fire as his patrol advances through the lanes and hedgerows of Normandy. He and his companion are armed with the MI carbines. Note also the wrecked German machine gun by his leg. (IWM - KY 27540)

landing beaches repairs to the Mulberry harbours had begun as soon as the storms abated on the 22nd; it was decided to combine what was left of them as one complete Mulberry at Arromanches. The storms had been so severe that they destroyed almost five times as many landing-craft as had German fire on D-Day! Meanwhile, in British Second Army's sector, regrouping was taking place in order for XXX, VIII and I Corps to be launched in a pincer movement on Caen (Operation 'Epsom'). The main initial thrust was in XXX Corps' sector, holding firm on the right and central sectors of the corps front, while advancing on the left to secure Noyers-Bocage. This would protect the right flank of VIII Corps which would be launched through Can 3rd Div, with the aim of seizing crossings over the Rivers Odon and Orne, to gain a position

on the high ground NE of Bretteville-sur-Laize which dominated the southern exits from Caen. The bad weather delayed operations and the attack had to be put off until 25 June. Some progress was made, but the enemy was well concealed in difficult country, with extensive minefields covering his positions, so by the end of 26 June leading troops had only reached Grainville-sur-Odon, Colleville and Mouen.

Week 4: 27 June–3 July 1944
The week began with the British/Canadian forces continuing Operation Epsom, their attempt to encircle Caen with VIII Corps, together with elements of I and XXX Corps, the first objective being the high ground around Hill 112, to the south-west of Caen. In a second phase the Allied forces would

Above: At 0730hrs on 26 June, an attack was put in by VIII Corps (15 Scottish, 43 Wessex and 11 Armd Divs), with 44 Bde of 15 Div opening the attack to capture St Mauvieu and La Gaule, two small villages south of Norrey-en-Bessin. Here, a section of 6 Royal Scots Fusiliers fire onto enemy positions from a sunken lane. (IWM - B 5959)

Above: A Canadian 7.2inch gun is prepared for action by its crew. Heavy guns like this were used mainly in counter-battery work against enemy artillery, 28 June 1944. (Public Archives Canada - PA 132925)

Right: Shermans belonging to Gen Le Clerc's 2nd French Armoured Division leave an LST on Utah Beach. The 2ème Division Blindée was then part of Patton's Third Army, which landed in early July 1944. (IWM - HU 73789)

advance eastwards across the River Orne. Once again the strength and fighting ability of the enemy proved too strong, and although a bridge-head over the Odon was secured, the road south-eastwards (known as 'Scotch Corridor') could not be held and Hill 112 was soon under heavy attack. By the 29th elements of seven panzer divisions were deployed against the bridge-head and Hill 112, resulting in the inevitable decision to cancel the second phase and withdraw. Nevertheless Montgomery ordered Second Army to maintain maximum pressure on the enemy, so as to ensure that the east flank remained firm. It was vital that the British/Canadian sector hold, so that enemy progress there would not be allowed to affect the overall Allied plan.

On the other flank, US troops completed the capture of Cherbourg on the 27th. The port was almost completely destroyed and it would take some time to be made operational. By the end of June, US 9th Division in the far west of the Cotentin peninsula had eliminated all enemy resistance – the entire peninsula was now virtually clear. By 30 June the Allies had

landed more than 630,000 troops, 600,000 tons of stores and 170,000 vehicles of all types. Allied casualty figures were about 1 in 10 killed or wounded. The week ended with US forces making a determined drive southwards (known as the 'Battle of the Hedgerows' from the nature of the thick bocage country with its sunken roads and high hedges) aiming towards the line Coutances–St-Lô. The weather was not good and little progress was made towards St-Jean-de-Daye and La-Haye-du-Puits. US First Army had just undergone a re-organisation, with VII Corps (4, 9 and 13 Divs) being moved to the sector between VIII and XIX Corps. As the week ended blinding rain continued to make progress slow.

Week 5: 4–10 July 1944

The slow advance continued on both flanks, both US VII and VIII Corps making some progress, while Can 1st Inf Div (part of British I Corps) captured Carpiquet to the west of Caen, but failed to take the nearby airfield in heavy fighting against 12th SS Pz Div. On 7 July Montgomery launched Operation 'Charn-

Above: Gen Omar Bradley celebrating the 4th of July. Promptly at noon on the 4th of July 1944, every American gun sent a shell screaming into German lines to celebrate Independence Day. Gen Bradley, then CG 1st US Army fired a 155m 'Long Tom' in the barrage. (IWM - EA 28821)

Right: Canadian soldiers having their breakfast in a slit-trench on the Caen-Carpiquet front, 9 July 1944. (Public Archives Canada - PA 131399)

Below: Canadian troops house-clearing in the outskirts of Caen, 10 July 1944, during hand-to-hand fighting. (Public Archives Canada - PA 132727)

wood', an attempt to take Caen from three sides, supported by massive bombing (some 2,000 tons of bombs were dropped and many civilians killed). The bombing created so much rubble that the advancing British and Canadian troops found their progress badly impeded, but by the 9th they had taken most of the city north of the Orne; the Germans still held the industrial area east of the river. Mopping-up continued on the 10th. In the city the bridges over the river were either destroyed or completely blocked by rubble. During the period 10–18 July, Second Army would deliver a series of thrusts, aimed at making progress southwards towards Thury-Harcourt on as broad a front as possible. These began on the 10th, with 43rd Div attacking the high ground at Point 112 and the villages of Feuguerolles-sur-Orne and Maltot in the Orne valley. All were secured, but a strong enemy counter-attack then retook Maltot.

Week 6: 11–17 July 1944

Throughout the week US First Army battled to capture St-Lô, which was the key to further advances southwards and an essential preliminary to their decisive breakout attack – code-named Operation 'Cobra', which would follow once St-Lô was taken. In the British sector there were advances towards Hottot-les-Bagues and Evrecy. In preparation for the forthcoming Operation 'Goodwood' considerable re-grouping took place, namely: during 12–13 July XII Corps took over from VIII Corps, and Can II Corps (Can 2nd and 3rd Inf Divs) became operational and took station between XII and I Corps. On 15 July XXX and XII Corps resumed the attack, the latter (a night attack on the 15th) being successfully supported for the first time by 'Movement Light' (searchlights directed at the clouds and then reflected downwards to give a degree of visibility). Some progress was made and, as mentioned already, Evrecy was taken, but fighting was severe and confused with many enemy armoured counter-attacks taking place. On the 17th, the Germans suffered a major reverse, in that Rommel was seriously wounded when his car was strafed while he was returning from a visit to SS Panzer General

'Sepp' Dietrich's HQ at St-Pierre-sur-Dives. He would play no further part in proceedings, his command responsibilities being taken over by Field Marshal Günther von Kluge, who had already taken over as CinC West from von Rundstedt.

Week 7: 18–24 July

18 July 1944. In the Cotentin peninsula, St-Lô was reached by US XIX Corps' troops. In the British sector Operation 'Goodwood' was launched. This was a massive tank attack by VIII Corps' armoured divisions to punch a

Above: German mines presented an ever-present hazard to the Allied soldier. Here a Canadian sapper uses his magnetic mine-detector which will sound a tell-tale 'beep' when it discovers something metal – a mine or just some scrap metal? Near Caen, 10 July 1944. (Public Archives Canada - PA 132856)

Above: Troops of US First Army assault enemy positions near St-Lô. Note the prone soldier about to fire his rifle grenade in support of their charge. (IWM - KY 30970)

Right: Tanks and infantry crossing the Odon River on the London Bailey Bridge, near Caen, 18 July 1944. (Public Archives - PA 131392)

LON

BRI

way through the strong German defences. It was preceded by a massive aerial bombardment by some 2,000 plus Allied aircraft dropping more than 7,000 tons of bombs. Montgomery considered that, even if the attack failed, it would take pressure off the American sector, in line with the overall plan; he was also under pressure to achieve some spectacular success on the British/Canadian front. The bombing, although it initially stunned the German defenders, did not destroy them, and the Allied tanks suffered heavily when they advanced towards the well-placed German anti-tank weapons. By the end of the day more than 200 Allied tanks had been destroyed, for a gain of less than six miles. The attack continued and by last light on the 19th the British had made some progress towards Bourguébus, while the Cana-

dians had taken the Caen suburbs of Vaucelles, Louvigny and Fleury-sur-Orne. Then the heavens opened, this time with torrential rain, and Goodwood ended on the 20th in a sea of mud and burning tanks. The weather also delayed the start of the US Operation 'Cobra', just west of St-Lô, air operations being impossible until the 25th when US VII Corps, supported by VIII Corps on its right and XIII Corps on its left, began its assault. The plan was for US First Army to pivot when it reached the base of the Cotentin peninsula and swing southwards, while VIII Corps swung west towards Rennes and St-Malo. General Patton's US Third Army, which by now was arriving in France and would be operational by 1 August, would then follow up, ready to take command of the breakout when ordered. Patton had made his usual

Above: Gen Montgomery holds his first press conference in Normandy, at which he explains the situation and progress of the landings to waiting journalists. (IWM - B 5339)

Above: General Montgomery together with US Generals Omar Bradley and George Patton, enjoy a joke. Relations between Monty and Patton were never particularly cordial, especially as each constantly strove to outdo the other. Note that Patton is wearing his famous ivory-handled pistols – not pearl-handled (he is reputed to have said that: '... only a pimp in a New Orleans whorehouse would have pearl grips!'). (IWM - B 6551)

spectacular arrival on the battle scene (on 6 July) at an airstrip near Omaha Beach and announced to waiting reporters that he was going to: '... cut the guts out of those Krauts and get the hell on to Berlin.'! 'Cobra' would have a bad start when bombs dropping short caused many Allied casualties, but both VII and VIII Corps would make good progress, vindicating the British and Canadian attacks at the other end of the front, which had undoubtedly drawn off many German tank units and other reserves.

The First 50 Days
Despite hard fighting, bad weather and other problems, the beach-head had been expanded and strengthened sufficiently for the next phase of operations to be launched, namely the breakout through France and on across the Seine. 'We were now on the threshold of great events,' Montgomery says in his memoirs. 'We were ready to break out of the bridge-head.'

Notes
1. Montgomery, B. *Normandy to the Baltic.*
2. The numbering of the weeks has been chosen purely arbitrarily in order to divide the text up into a logical pattern of seven-day periods. The original D-Day was to have been Monday 5 June, but was postponed until Tuesday 6 June. Therefore I have taken my seven-day 'weeks' as starting on a Tuesday and ending on a Monday – and of course Week 1 began with D-Day.
3. The Allied tank with the best firepower was the Sherman 'Firefly' armed with the British 17pdr, but only a small number was available at the time.

Left: 'Kamerad'! This German sniper was only fourteen years old and was captured by the Americans in Normandy. For him the fighting is over. (US Army)

Below: Captured German troops were brought down to the beaches and shipped off in returning LSLs to POW camps in UK and elsewhere, staging through temporary POW cages at places like Portland in Dorset. (IWM - MH 9102)

3

Breakout

Below: Excellent photograph taken during Winston Churchill's visit to the Caen area on 22 July 1944. He drove over two bridges across the River Orne built by the REs – 'Winston Bridge' and 'Churchill Bridge' – and talked with both British and Canadian troops. Here, accompanied by Gen Sir Bernard Montgomery and Gen Sir Miles Dempsey, he looks at a map on which Lt Gen Symonds (commander 2nd Canadian Corps) is pointing out enemy positions. (IWM - B 7879)

Résumé of the Plan

Having established a secure beach-head on the Normandy coast and consolidated their troops within it, it was now time for the Allies to move on to the next phase of operations, namely to break out from the confines of the Cotentin peninsula, gain control of Brittany and then swing wide to the east across France. On the left flank, the British and Canadian armies would continue to mount attacks with the aim of containing as many German forces as possible and masking the main effort, which would be made by the Americans on the right. The latter would pivot on the left flank and swing south on the right, thus securing the whole of the Cotentin peninsula. On reaching the base of the peninsula, VIII

Corps would turn west into Brittany, making for Rennes and St-Malo. US Third Army would follow on their extreme right, ready to take command of the breakout when ordered. US First Army's operation was known as 'Cobra' and H-Hour had been set for 1300 hrs on 24 July, but then postponed for 24 hours because of bad flying weather. Heavy saturation bombing and artillery barrages preceded the attack.

Week 8: 25–31 July 1944

US First Army's Operation 'Cobra' began on the 25th. The massive air and artillery preparation included some 1,500 heavy bombers of US Eighth Army Air Force. Bombs landing short caused many casualties, which included

Above: Cromwell tanks and M10 tank destroyers of 22nd Armd Bde, lined up before an attack east of the River Orne, late July 1944. (Tank Museum)

Lieutenant General Lesley J. McNair, CG US Army Ground Forces, who was visiting the front. Despite this initial setback both VII and VIII Corps made good progress, which they continued on the 26th, US VII Corps taking Marigny and St-Gilles, and west of them VIII Corps was across the Lessay–Périers road. By the 29th, XIX Corps on the far left of the assault was advancing towards Torigny and Tessy, while VII Corps had reached Percy and on the right VIII Corps was across the River Sienne and pushing towards Granville. They entered Avranches the next day, seizing vital bridges over the River Sée. On the left flank of the advance the enemy counter-attacked strongly around Percy and Villedieu. This was the pattern for the next day's fighting; on the right US 4th Armd Div striking out from Avranches and capturing crossings over the River Sélune near Pontaubault, while on the left flank determined resistance continued.

Farther east, in the British/Canadian sector, British Second Army regrouped and, towards the end of the week, began a thrust south-wards from the Caumont area. The main weight of the attack was to be on a narrow front in VIII and XXX Corps' area, wheeling south-west then developing eastwards towards the Orne. The attack began on XXX Corps' front at 0600 hrs of 30 July, 43rd Inf Div's task being to secure the hill feature Point 361 to the west of Jurques, while 50th Div aimed to secure the high ground west of Villers-Bocage. The VIII Corps attack was timed to start an hour later, with 11th Armd and 15th Inf Divs being ordered to establish themselves in the area of St-Martin-des-Besaces, protecting the right flank of XXX Corps. Progress in VIII Corps' area proved easier than on XXX Corps' front and the attacks were continued on 31 July, gains being made although opposition was by now stiffening. In Can II Corps' area south of Caen, good progress was also made towards Tilly-la-Campagne and Bourguébus.

Allied casualty figures to the end of July were some 122,000 killed and wounded; the Germans had lost about 154,000 (including 40,000 taken prisoner). The week closed with Patton's US Third Army, now assembled and poised to become operational and take over the Allied right flank. US forces were re-organised into 12th Army Group (under General

Above: 1st (US) Army launch Operation 'Cobra'. An American patrol makes its way carefully through the ruins of St-Lô towards Notre Dame Cathedral, 25 July 1944. (US Army via Real War Photos A-329)

Right: With British forces south of Caumont, 31 July 1944. They even had traffic jams in the front line! This lane is very congested with infantry-filled carriers, all trying to get forward. (IWM - B 8308)

Above: Seaforth High-landers, supported by half-tracks, carriers and tanks on the road to Vassy, north of Flers, 2 August 1944. (IWM - B 8603)

Bradley) containing First Army (General Hodges) and Third Army (Patton); the British/Canadian 21st Army Group comprised Canadian First Army (General Crerar) and British Second Army (General Dempsey), still under Montgomery's command who also retained overall command of all ground forces.

Week 9: 1–7 August 1944

When US Third Army became operational – at 1200 hrs, Tuesday, 1 August – it assumed operational control over all troops in US VIII Corps' zone, so Patton now had under his command four corps: VIII Corps (General Middleton), XV Corps (General Haislip), XX Corps (General Walker) and XII Corps (General Cook). The plan for the coming month's operations would be developed in five phases: the conquest of Brittany; the encirclement of German Seventh Army in the Argentan–Falaise–Mortain area; the advance to the River Seine, to include the enveloping of

all enemy forces from Mantes Gassicourt to Elbeuf; forcing the enemy to evacuate south-western France; routing the enemy across the Rivers Marne, Aisne and Meuse. Patton was of course the ideal commander for such a dynamic, fast-moving series of operations. One of the cornerstones of the Allied cover plan (Operation 'Fortitude') had been to persuade the enemy that he was commanding a mythical army group located in SE England, which would form the major assault force in the Pas-de-Calais.[1] Uncertain what to expect and riven by command problems, the Germans were unable to present a cohesive front line although they did manage to establish some solid defensive localities with well-emplaced artillery support. But Third Army's armoured spearheads burst out of Avranches and made considerable progress to the south, taking Rennes on 3 August and, in the south-east, capturing Mayenne on the 5th. To the west a special armoured Task Force made for

Right: A typical British section, led by its section commander (with Sten SMG), Bren gunner and riflemen. They belonged to 9 Platoon, A Coy, 1/5 Bn Welch Regiment. (IWM - B8919)

Below: The advance towards Aunay-sur-Odon. Men of the Worcestershire Regiment search for snipers in ruined houses near Benneville. 2 August 1944. (IWM - B 8501)

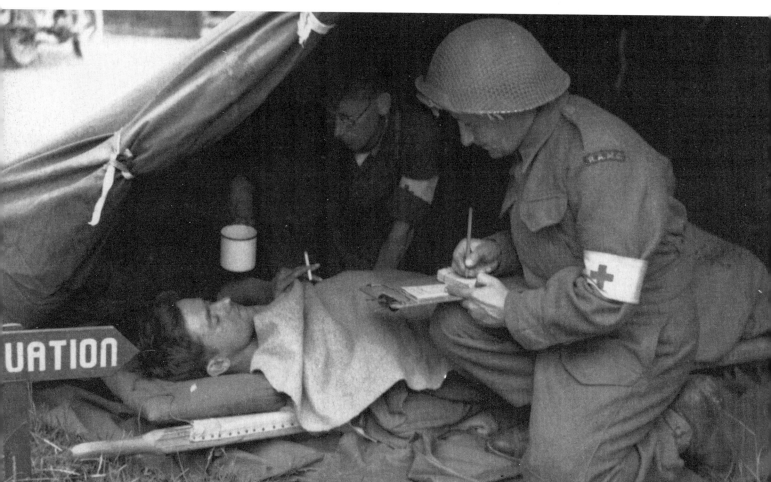

Left: Attack on the Odon Valley. British 5.5inch medium guns firing a night barrage, which began the attack on the river valley area. (IWM - B 7413)

Right: One of the leading armored divisions of Patton's 3rd Army was Maj Gen 'Tiger Jack' Wood's 4th Armd Div. Always a thrusting commander, 'Tiger Jack' is seen here in an M8 Greyhound armoured car at Avranches. (US Army via Patton Museum)

Left: A casualty enjoys a cigarette and a cuppa, whilst waiting to be taken to a field hospital from an ad hoc casevac point. (IWM - B 6838)

Right: Excellent shot of a self-propelled howitzer, belonging to 'B' Battery, 22nd Armd Field Artillery Bn, 4th Armd Div, 3rd (US) Army seen here moving through Coutances. The HMC M7 mounted a 105mm M1A2 howitzer and was known as the Priest in British Army service. (US Army via Patton Museum)

Above: The Battle for St-Lô. Litter bearers bring wounded GIs to a 1st Army regimental aid station. (US Army via Real War Photos A - 353)

Brest, capturing Vannes on the 5th, with VIII Corps following up. Brest was reached on the 7th but the garrison refused to surrender (they would hold out until 19 September!). Patton's spearheads had excellent, close air protection from General Weyland's XIX Tactical Air Command. During August and on into September 1944, they inflicted devastating damage on the enemy by, for example, attacking ground targets in direct support of armour and infantry, providing air cover for columns and assaults, area patrols and armed recce, pre-planned point target attacks (dive-bombing) in much the same way as the Luft-waffe had supported the panzer divisions in the heady *Blitzkrieg* days of the 'France 1940' assault. The boot was now very firmly on the other foot! By nightfall on the 6th Patton's troops had already liberated some 3½ million people in 119 towns and villages.

US First Army was also making progress southwards, taking Villedieu on the 2nd and Mortain on the 3rd. As they pressed steadily beyond Mortain, the Germans mounted a counter-attack with 2nd and 116th Pz Divs just to the east, and on the 7th they retook the town. It rapidly became clear that this was a major enemy assault (code-named Operation 'Lüttich'). The German High Command had realised that the most critical moment in the battle for Normandy had now been reached; indeed they considered that this was now such an important battle that it could well decide the outcome of the struggle for western Europe and possibly of the entire war. Hitler had personally ordered that the panzer divisions should be formed up outside Mortain, facing westwards and then launched in an attack which was to drive down the Rivers Sée and Sélune to reach the sea at Avranches. However, despite the costly battles which had occurred along the River Odon in July, Hitler and his staff did not realise that armoured operations of this magnitude could not be successful without complete air superiority. The German field commanders fully appreciated the danger, but were unable to persuade von Kluge to rescind Hitler's orders. Despite heavy enemy pressure, the Tactical Air Forces and American counter-measures repulsed the attacks in the

Right: The Battle for St-Lô. 1st Army traffic moving through the ruins of St-Lô, 2 August 1944. (US Army via Real War Photos A- 314)

Below: 3rd Army breakout. Main 'player' in the breakout was of course the CG 3rd Army – Lt Gen George S. Patton, Jr, seen here studying a battle map with Maj Gen Hugh Gaffey, his Chief of Staff, watched by Maj M. C. Helfers, Special Intelligence Officer on operations of the German forces opposing the American thrust. (US Army)

Left: Monty visits the 1st Polish Armoured Division, 6 August 1944. Here he meets a number of Polish officers and is introduced to them by Maj Gen Maczek, the GOC. (IWM B8762)

Below: British troops advance south of Le Beny Bocage. Moving through typical bocage hedgerows, where an ambush can lurk around every corner, 6 August 1944. (Bruce Robertson)

Above: Nice to meet you!. American and British troops meet for the first time as the two armies link up on the Argentan road, August 1944. (IWM - HU 43955)

Below: Heavy fighting in progress in the area between Caen and Falaise, August 1944. (IWM - HU 3021)

Above: This massive Royal Tiger tank was knocked out on 7 August 1944, near Le Plosis Grimault. Fortunately the Germans only built 489 of these 68 ton heavy tanks, whose 88mm gun could easily deal with its opponents at ranges where their own armour was virtually impenetrable. (Tank Museum)

Left: Winnie visits Monty. Prime Minister Winston Churchill paid numerous flying visits to Normandy, this time on 7 August 1944. Here he meets one of Monty's new puppies called 'Rommel'! (IWM - B 8766)

Right: Vehicles belonging to the 3rd Canadian Division, photographed during the 'mad dash' period of Operation 'Tractable', as they pour forward near Bretteville-le-Rabet, 14 August 1944. (National Archives of Canada - PA 116536)

Above: Canadian
soldiers move past a
burning ammunition
truck during Operation
'Totalize', the Canadian
breakout, which also
involved British and
Polish troops, 8 August
1944. (National Archives
of Canada - PA 131375)

Mortain area. During the night of the 7th,
Canadian forces south-west of Caen also
advanced, assisted by more than 1,000 RAF
bombers which dropped some 3,000 plus tons
of bombs on the enemy pushing towards
Falaise. The German defences here were formidable, so the plan was to assault under cover of
darkness, with the infantry in heavy armoured
carriers (these were gutted 'Sexton' SP gun
carriages which came to be known as 'Kanga-
roos'). Initially the attack went well and by
midday on the 8th the villages of May-sur-
Orne, Fontenay and Tilly-la-Campagne had

been taken. The Canadians then came up
against a very strong lay-back position astride
the high ground.

Week 10: 8–14 August 1944

The only remaining aggressive enemy resistance in US Third Army's area was against VIII
Corps at St-Malo which had been heavily fortified and the harbour locks mined, but by the
14th only the ancient citadel in the port area
remained in enemy hands. The leading
elements of XV Corps were now only twelve
miles from Le Mans, the enemy offering only

Left: A vital task during the advance – and at all other times for that matter – was that of artillery observation officers, who directed the fire of the field artillery onto enemy positions from their often exposed OPs. This one was operating near Barenton, France on 10 August 1944. (IWM - EA 51085)

Below: British and Canadian tanks form up for Operation 'Tractable', 14 August 1944. Nearest the camera appears to be an M10 tank destroyer. This open-topped TD mounted a 3in gun on the Sherman chassis. Another version was the M10 Achilles, which mounted the British 17pdr. Behind the M10 is a Churchill flame-thrower, towing its trailer full of flame fluid. (National Archives of Canada - PA 116525)

token resistance; XII and XX Corps were advancing on Orléans and Chartres.

The major trouble spot for the Allies was still around Mortain, where the struggle continued. The Germans were still trying to make their major breakthrough, but they were held, then gradually worn down, so that by the 11th even von Kluge was more than anxious to withdraw his forces while they were still reasonably intact; he was prevented from doing so by Hitler who would only allow a partial withdrawal. Farther south, US forces had crossed the River Loire. To the north-east, by the 14th, the Canadians were only about five miles from Falaise, and still getting massive air support from the RAF. On the administrative front, the first PLUTO was brought into operation on 12 August, carrying fuel from the Isle of Wight to Cherbourg. Eventually no less than 20 such pipelines were laid under the Channel from the Isle of Wight and Dungeness to Cherbourg and Boulogne respectively.

Week 11: 15–21 August 1944
(See Chapter 4 for the Operation 'Dragoon' landings on 16 August and the subsequent advance northwards up the Rhône valley.)

Right: Bonjour Americans! French citizens of Angers crowd into the narrow streets of Angers to welcome XX Corps troops, who entered the town on 12 August. (IWM EA - 33103)

Lower right: The 'Funnies' of 79th Armoured Division, taking part in Operation 'Tractable', 14 August 1944, near Bretteville-le-Rabet. Both are Churchill AVREs; the one on the left is carrying a brushwood fascine which was dropped into trenches/ditches to assist the tank in crossing. The 290mm Petard spigot mortar demolition gun can be clearly seen on the other AVRE. (National Archives of Canada - PA 116523)

On the 15th, SHAEF announced that US Third Army was now operating in France and 12th Army Group ordered Patton to hold the southern sector of the Argentan–Falaise gap with XV Corps, together with VII Corps (First Army), while simultaneously making a rapid movement eastwards to harass and confuse the enemy. The objective of XX Corps was changed from Dreux to Chartres. By now the area south of the Seine from Paris to Orléans was under US Third Army's control. Dreux was captured by XV Corps on the 16th and XII Corps took Orléans on the same day. Patton then ordered XII Corps to hold Orléans with a small force, move the bulk of the corps south of Janville and press on eastwards. By the 18th

Below: British tanks and anti-tank guns moving forward in the Argentan area, during August 1944. (Bruce Robertson)

Left: Canadian tanks move up for their role in Operation 'Totalize'. Note the extra protection afforded to the Sherman in the right of the track, by the track plates welded to the front glacis. The Sherman, despite being a good all-round medium tank, was known as the 'Ronson Lighter' by its crews as it was: '... guaranteed to light first time!' (National Archives of Canada - PA 132904)

Right: Street fighting in Falaise. Infantry-tank co-operation had to be of a very high order. Here infantry of Les Fusiliers Mont-Royal get support from a Sherman of the Sherbrooke Fusiliers during a sniper hunt on 17 August 1944. (National Archives of Canada - PA 115568)

Right: GIs of 83rd Infantry Division dealing with enemy snipers in house-to-house fighting in St-Malo, 17 August 1944. (US Army)

they had secured bridge-heads over the River Eure at Dreux and Chartres and were closing up on the Seine. On the 20th, XX Corps established bridge-heads across the river and launched attacks east of the Seine at Mellun and Fontainebleau. On 21st Army Group's front, British VIII Corps entered Tinchebray on the 15th, while other British and Canadian units were attacking towards Falaise, Can 2nd Inf Div capturing the town on the 17th. To their south, US VII and V Corps were pushing northwards in an endeavour to trap units of Fifth Panzer Army and Seventh Army between them, the enemy trying desperately to escape the pincers. The 'Falaise Gap' was closed on the 18th by a conjunction of Polish and US

Above: The top brass at work in France, August 1944. L to R: Gen Sir Miles Dempsey (2nd Br Army), Gen Courtney Hodges (1st US Army), Gen Henry Crerar (Can 1st Army), Gen Sir Bernard Montgomery (21st Army Group) and Gen Omar Bradley (12th US Army Group). (IWM - B9674)

Left: Commander of the 1st Polish Armoured Division, Maj Gen Stanislaw Maczek, talking with Canadian war correspondents, following the Poles' heroic defence of position 'Maczuga' (mace), plugging the gap to bottle up German armour in the Falaise Pocket. (National Archives of Canada - PA 129140)

Above: Polish tank crewmen talk with Sgt McVay of the Black Watch, south of Caen. It was men like this who plugged the Falaise Gap and prevented large numbers of German tanks from escaping. (IWM - B 8829)

armoured units at Chambois. There were still considerable German forces west of the Gap and Allied fighter-bombers had a field-day, knocking out many tanks and other AFVs. Nevertheless a number of the remaining panzer units did manage to escape during the night of the 20th. (In all from 19 to 29 August, some 300,000 enemy soldiers and 25,000 vehicles managed to escape, but they left behind 50,000 dead, 200,000 prisoners and the wreckage of precious vehicles and equipment which had once equipped two armies. One estimate of total German tank losses during the Normandy campaign was 1,300-plus; *Panzer Lehr*, 9th Pz Div and some fifteen infantry divisions virtually ceased to exist.

Another 'casualty' of the disastrous Mortain counter-attack was the German commander FM von Kluge. He had been visiting the Falaise area on 12 August when his vehicle was hit by artillery fire and he was pinned down in a ditch for some twelve hours. Hitler, assuming that he had deserted, sent FM Model to replace him, and when Kluge re-appeared he was

ordered back to Germany 'for a rest'. Von Kluge, fearing the worst, took poison and died near Metz on the 19th, leaving a message which professed undying personal loyalty to his Führer. After a short time it became clear that running both OB West and Army Group B was beyond Model's abilities, so Hitler recalled von Rundstedt (see later), leaving Model to re-organise the shattered Army Group, which he did most effectively.

Week 12: 22–28 August 1944

All Allied armies began a rapid advance north-eastwards in pursuit of the disorganised German forces. At 0700 hrs on 25 August, French 2nd Armd Div, which had been released from all other duties (on Eisenhower's direct orders) so that it could have the honour of liberating France's capital, entered Paris from the south-west. Half an hour later, US 4th Inf Div did likewise from the south. Fortunately the German Garrison commander, General von Choltitz, ignored Hitler's order to blow up the main public buildings, bridges

Above: American engineers dropping the last section of a pontoon treadway bridge into position, across the River Seine, west of Paris. (Tank Museum)

Left: Half-tracks, followed by trucks of 3rd Armd Div of 1st (US) Army, crossing the Seine on 26 August 1944. (US Army via Real War Photos - A 661A)

and monuments, and at 1515 hrs surrendered the city to General Leclerc, relatively undamaged and with little fighting. General de Gaulle returned to Paris the following day and took part in a large ceremonial parade. To the north of Paris, British 43rd Inf Div established a bridge-head over the Seine at Vernon, and downriver at Louviers near Rouen British XII Corps did likewise. On the same day three divisions of US VIII Corps (2nd, 80th and 90th) began a major assault against Brest after another aerial bombardment. By the 26th most of the Allied armies had units across the Seine with US Third Army leading the charge, taking Château-Thierry on the Marne on the 27th, as well as reaching Troyes, farther south on the Seine. On the 28th US First Army had units across the Marne at Meaux, and US Third Army was approaching Rheims. In the north, having crossed the lower Seine on the 26th, Canadian First Army moved towards Calais, while British Second Army units made for Belgium. On the 27th British I Corps reached the mouth of the Seine and the following day Can II Corps expanded its bridge-head towards Rouen.

Notes

1. Patton had apparently 'disappeared' after Sicily and, because the Germans rated him as the best Allied armoured commander, it seemed to them only logical that he had been given this important role – they hadn't realised that the notorious 'slapping incident' in Sicily had been taken so seriously by 'the powers that be'. 'I'm not supposed to be commanding this Army,' he would gleefully tell his troops during his 'pep-talks' in the UK prior to the invasion. 'I'm not even supposed to be in England. Let the first bastards to find out be the Goddamn Germans. I want them to look up and howl: "Ach, it's the Goddamn Third Army and that son-of-a-bitch Patton again!"'

Below: As the Allies raced across France, the French insurgent forces (FFI = Forces Françaises de l'Intérieur) came out into the open. (Author's Collection)

Left: Gen Phiippe Leclerc, CG 2nd French Armd Div, whose division was rightly given the honour of being the first Allied troops to enter Paris. (Author's Collection)

Below: Thousands of Parisians encircle the Champs Elysées to witness the victory parade on 26 August 1944. Gen Charles de Gaulle, president of the French Committee of National Liberation, led the parade, followed by units of LeClerc's 2nd French Armd Div. (Author's Collection)

Right: RAF rocket-firing Typhoons were responsible for knocking out this German armour south-east of Coutances, having been 'invited' to take part by American army chiefs. By the end of the day they had destroyed 32 enemy tanks as well as numerous other AFVs and wheeled transport. (Air Ministry Photograph CL 631 XP)

Right: After the capture of Avranches, American armoured forces continued to push south and east, as Patton's spearheads swept through France. These German POWs were part of 20,000 captured in the battle for Avranches. (US Army)

Right: Captured German troops in Paris are marched through the streets, much to the delight of crowds of derisive Parisians. (Author's Collection)

Above: Members of the FFI (Forces Françaises de l'Intérieur) have linked up with friendly forces during the Allied race across France. These two young Frenchmen wear the FFI armband, bearing the Cross of Lorraine. The young man in the helmet is certainly well armed – he has a British Sten gun and a German P38 pistol in a Type 1 holster as well as his rifle! The other wears a German leather belt with the SS buckle (upside down) adorned with a spread eagle clutching a swastika. (IWM - BU 217)

Above: 'Vive les Anglais!" Mde Scarlette of Les Andelys on the River Seine proudly wears her Union Jack blouse as she waves to troops passing by her Hôtel des Fleurs, 31 August 1944. (IWM - B 9869)

Below: Not only did they get rid of the enemy, some GIs also helped to bring in the harvest. These American soldiers are helping 'down on the farm' near St-Malo soon after its capture. (IWM - EA 36504)

4

Operation 'Dragoon'

A second 'Second Front'

As has been mentioned, a long-standing argument had continually affected American-British relations, concerning where the 'Second Front' should be mounted. Churchill, worried about a possible takeover of central and eastern Europe by the Communists, was very much in favour of reinforcing Allied operations in Italy and striking up through the Balkans, into Austria and Hungary, to take Vienna and Budapest, then on across the Danube into southern Germany, thus thwarting Stalin's now rampant Red Army of many of its spoils of victory. Unfortunately, the Americans did not agree; they disliked Churchill's 'Balkan intrigues' and did not want to sacrifice American lives for the sake of what

they saw as merely securing the *status quo* in Europe. They would of course live to regret their decision post-war, but having won their case that 'Overlord' should take place in northern France, they now opted for a second 'Second Front' in the South of France. Stalin was delighted and continued to support what some American/British cynics called 'The Stalin Plan'; as far as he was concerned it could take place anywhere, preferably as far west as possible but certainly not in the Balkans! Eventually Churchill gave in and 'Anvil', as it was then called (later changed to 'Dragoon'), was scheduled to take place at the same time as 'Overlord', so as to draw enemy troops away from the main Allied assault. This proposal was thwarted because there just weren't

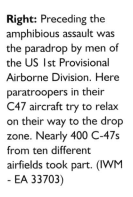

Right: Preceding the amphibious assault was the paradrop by men of the US 1st Provisional Airborne Division. Here paratroopers in their C47 aircraft try to relax on their way to the drop zone. Nearly 400 C-47s from ten different airfields took part. (IWM - EA 33703)

enough landing-craft to mount both operations simultaneously; after various postponements it was agreed that Operation 'Dragoon' would take place on 15 August 1944. The chosen location was to be in Provence, east of Marseilles, between Toulon and Cannes. The assaulting force would be under the command of Major General Alexander M. Patch's US Seventh Army, whose HQ was then at Naples. Its amphibious landing force was to be composed of Major General Lucian K. Truscott's US VI Corps (US 3rd, 36th and 45th Inf Divs). This would land first and be followed by General de Lattre de Tassigny's French *Armée B* (to be renamed French First Army a month later), a force of some 256,000 men, comprising seven French divisions, including troops from the French Expeditionary Corps and their *Armée d'Afrique*.[1] The amphibious assault would be preceded by a paradrop by US 1st Provisional Airborne Division. The landings would be watched by

Churchill and General Maitland 'Jumbo' Wilson, who was CinC Mediterranean and thus nominally in charge of the operation although he had passed responsibility down to his deputy, US General Jacob Devers. Opposing the landing were elements of General Blaskowitz's Army Group G, although only three of his ten divisions were located near the chosen beaches. As with 'Overlord', the Allies would have massive air and naval superiority, although there was a shortage of landing-craft, and no specialised armour such as had been so successful on D-Day would take part.

The Landings

Supported by some 880 warships of the Western Naval Task Force, which included five battleships, 21 cruisers and 100 destroyers, more than 1,400 landing-craft took part in the amphibious landings on 15 August 1944, the fleet coming from five ports

Above: With text-book precision, the paradrop was completed successfully near Oraguigan and Le Muy, the first stick jumping at 0430hrs. There was only one serious error, when, due to low-lying fog, one battalion was dropped some 20 miles from its assigned DZ. (IWM - EA 33702)

Above: Watching the landings in southern France was the British Prime Minister Winston Churchill, on board the destroyer *Kimberley*, flagship of Admiral Sir John Cunningham. Churchill would coerce the destroyer's skipper to get far closer to the beaches than he should (due to the dangers from hundreds of floating mines). (IWM - A 25254)

Right: Landing craft approaching the beaches. Most GIs seem to be wearing the issue inflatable lifebelts, but otherwise appear to be casually watching the shore through binoculars – no 'incoming' by the look of things. (IWM - IA 33990)

of embarkation in Italy, Sicily and North Africa, to rendezvous opposite their appointed beaches, between Fréjus and Cannes, having first headed towards northern Italy, to disguise their true destination. Overhead there were continual sorties by the 2,000 aircraft which the Allies had concentrated on airfields in Corsica and Sardinia, and on nine aircraft carriers – outnumbering the Luftwaffe by at least 10 to 1! While the invasion fleet was assembling, the airborne element, transported in almost 400 C-47s from ten airfields in Italy, had been successfully dropped near Draguignan and le Muy, the first stick jumping at 0430 hrs. At the same time, a few aircraft had dropped hundreds of small dummy parachutists in the Toulon area to confuse the enemy. Low-lying

fog hampered some of the paratroop drops and one battalion was dropped some 20 miles away from the assigned drop zones. But this was the only serious error, the remainder of 1st Airborne Task Force landing according to plan. The follow-up glider force landed near le Muy some five hours later, more than 70 gliders bringing in artillery, anti-tank guns and small vehicles. Towards last light a further 330 plus gliders arrived, so that by the end of the day some 9,000 Allied airborne troops had been landed, with more than 200 artillery pieces and an equivalent number of vehicles. Losses had been slight – 434 killed and 292 injured. They were now ready to assault the enemy at le Muy.

Despite considerable quantities of mines and other beach obstacles, which had to be

Below: Unloading from this landing craft on 15 August is a Multiple Gun Motor Carriage M15A1, which had a 37mm cannon and two .50 cal machine guns in a combination mount. The half-track belonged to 3rd Inf Div. (US Army via Real War Photos A-2512)

Above: Allied troops advancing through a smokescreen, having debarked from landing craft, whilst a fair number of German prisoners (in the centre of the photograph) are being corralled together. (IWM - NYF 37154)

Below: Follow-up troops of 45th Inf Div wade ashore on Camel Beach. The leading GIs are carrying a disassembled 81mm mortar. (IWM - NYF 40310)

Left: A column of American infantrymen move past two DUKW – or to give their full designation: 2ton 6x6 Amphibian Truck GMC DUKW 353. They mount 57mm anti-tank guns and were often so employed during beach assaults. (IWM - IAP 33982)

Left: US engineers crossing the bridge at St-Raphael after its capture. The seaside town, which was near Camel Red Beach, had some of its waterfront bars, kiosks and bathing cabins disguising coastal gun positions. (IWM - IA 35339)

Left: Men of 3rd Infantry Division crossing the River Doubs in Besançon, during the push northwards, 8 September 1944. (US Army via Real War Photos A-2495)

Above: GIs of 143rd Regt 36 Inf Div ride on one of their tank battalion Shermans through this French town, whilst the people cheer them on, 16 September 1944. (US Army via Real War Photos - A 3297)

cleared by underwater demolition teams, the amphibious landings were also achieved with only minimal casualties (fewer than 200 killed), thanks to the preliminary heavy air and sea bombardment and the lack of immediate heavy enemy opposition. Three beach areas had been chosen – from west to east: 3rd Inf Div landing on 'Alpha', 45th Inf Div on 'Delta' and 36th Inf Div on 'Camel', with on the left French Commandos whose job it was to cut the road to Toulon. The 1st Special Service Force (US and Can Commandos) was sent to silence heavy German guns on the Iles d'Hyères, which critically overlooked Alpha Beach, but on arrival, the guns were found to be dummies. The stiffest fighting was on Camel, against heavy and accurate fire which could not be silenced by the sea bombardment. Eventually, however, the troops made it ashore and consolidated their beach-head.

As planned, on the 16th, General de Tassigny's II Corps (which landed from D+1 to D+25) passed through the Americans and took over the coastal advance, making for the main initial targets, namely the ports of Toulon and

Marseilles, both of which were heavily defended. The Americans advanced inland on the right flank, with 36th Inf Div heading for the valley of the Durance and 3rd and 45th Inf Divs going for Aix-en-Provence (taken 21 August) and Avignon (25 August). The German garrisons at Toulon and Marseilles fought stubbornly and it took the French colonial forces some twelve days to capture both the key ports which had been designated as 'fortresses of no surrender' by Hitler. Nearly 48,000 prisoners were taken in the two fortresses. French I Corps, which had landed behind II Corps, had crossed the Rhône and turned northwards on 28 August. The race was now on to link up with Patton's Third Army well to the north. Operation 'Dragoon' had been an unqualified success. In total some 380,000 men, 69,000 vehicles and 306,000 tons of supplies were landed between 16 August and 2 September.

With the Germans withdrawing in front of them, the US and French forces pressed northwards. On the right, Grenoble was taken on 24 August and on the left Lyons on 3 September.

Above: Historic meeting of US Third and Seventh Armies, 12 September 1944, in Autun, France. The two M8 Greyhound armoured cars were driven by Dvr Jean Quigon (left) who had advanced northwards from Toulon and Cpl Carl Newman, 86th Recon Sqn of the US Sixth Armd Div, one of Patton's hard-driving armoured divisions. Here, Sgt Louis Basil, the Greyhound commander, shakes hands with the French driver. (4/15 is IWM - EA 37766. 4/16 is Author's Collection)

Below: Remnants of the German First Army endeavoured, with some success, to get through the Belfort Gap to escape into Germany, whilst the Seventh US and First French Armies tried to prevent them. Here a Sherman tank belonging to a French armoured unit opens up onto an enemy position on the outskirts of Belfort. (IWM - EA 44782)

Above: A machine gunner of the 1st French Army turns his .30 Browning MG, on its ground mounting, onto an enemy position in Belfort as they liberated this key town. (IWM - EA 44813)

Right: Two French soldiers of a signal team of the 3rd Algerian Infantry Division, plus their wire-laden mule, move up in the foothills of the Vosges Mountains, in a new Allied drive towards the German frontier. (IWM - EA 42953)

Towards the end, the Germans chose to fight one final delaying action at Besançon in order to try to gain a breathing-space to withdraw the bulk of what was left of their forces through the Belfort Gap. Some 3,000 enemy were in position there and a fierce fight developed for control of Besançon. On the left, French II Corps advanced northwards from Lyons, liberating Dijon on 10 September and taking many thousands of prisoners.[2] On 12 September the first contacts were made between units of General Leclerc's Free French 2nd Armd Div, serving with Patton's Third Army, which had fought its way from Normandy, via Paris, with the advance elements of French II Corps, in the area of Châtillon-sur-Seine. A fair number of German troops had managed to escape at various places along the route and they were able

eventually to join up with Army Group B, but they had taken heavy losses, thanks to Allied artillery and air strikes, in particular against General von Wietersheim's 11th Pz Div. In addition, some 80,000 prisoners were taken. German First Army, under General von der Chevallerie, had also now withdrawn from south-west France. The Allied aim had been achieved and the front was now continuous from the English Channel in the north to Switzerland in the south.

Notes

1. General de Lattre de Tassigny had made a strong case for the French to land first, but was overruled.
2. A large proportion of these were East European 'volunteer' units, who killed their officers and went over to the Allied side.

Above: Residents of Belfort march along with the Second Moroccan Infantry Division band as they celebrate their liberation. 20 November 1944. (IWM - EA 45330)

5

From the Seine to the Rhine

Below: Spoils of war. Men of the 734th US Ordnance Battalion, of Seventh Army, dragging an apparently undamaged PzKpfw III Ausf L, off the battlefield in late August 1944, using their wrecker, which bears the standard national identification symbol on its door. Note the heavy machine gun cal .50 on a ring-mount over the cab. (Tank Museum)

A Strategic Dilemma

Poised astride the Seine, with the new 'push' from the 'Dragoon' landings making good progress up the Rhône valley, it was now time to liberate the rest of France and take the battle into the Low Countries. However, an increasingly acrimonious argument had been raging for some time between the Allied senior commanders as to how best to proceed with the overall strategic battle. The two main opposing arguments posited either a broad advance with all the armies sharing supplies (and glory!), or a bolder, swift advance on a much narrower front, with a much smaller force. Eisenhower, ever the careful diplomat, favoured the broad approach, reasoning that the more cautious advance, with all armies keeping roughly in line, would be safer, easier to handle and a much better way of keeping the peace between such fiery characters as Patton and Montgomery. They of course, especially Montgomery, who was promoted to Field Marshal on 31 August, favoured the narrow thrust. His plan was for a bold advance by some 20 divisions which would smash their way into Germany, encircle the Ruhr and end the war at a stroke. They would of course get the lion's share of fuel and *matériel* while everyone else waited for more supplies to become available. While he was happy that it

Left: French children and their mothers wave to the crews of a column of Polish tanks as they enter the village of Pommeroy. (Author's Collection)

Left: Polish tank crewmen are pictured here on their appropriately named Sherman. Gen Mazcek's armoured division fought valiantly throughout the North-West European campaign. (Author's Collection)

should be a mixed Allied strike force, it was quite clear who was to command it! 'My own view, which I presented to the Supreme Commander,' he wrote in his memoirs, 'was that one powerful full-blooded thrust across the Rhine and into the heart of Germany, backed by the whole of the resources of the Allied armies, would be likely to achieve decisive results.' Monty outlined two routes for such an advance: the northernmost through Belgium to the Rhine, crossing north of the Ruhr industrial region and into the open plains of northern Germany; alternatively, through Metz, the Saar and into central Germany. He naturally favoured the northern route!

Eisenhower did not want to rock the boat, but he feared, with some justification, that the narrow approach was just too vulnerable and might well be cut off. The German armies were not completely beaten and still presented a considerable threat, especially as they were

Right: A large Canadian soldier chats to a small member of the FFI, who cradles his Sten – fortunately with the cocking lever in the safety position! (IWM - HU 28887)

Below: Members of the FFI wave a greeting to a column of British tanks, led by a Sherman Firefly (mounting the British 17pdr gun instead of the normal 75mm). (IWM - HU 73714)

being driven back into their home territory, and would fight ever more fiercely to protect the Fatherland. With hindsight, and especially taking into consideration the overwhelming Allied air superiority, he was probably being overcautious, though everyone would be caught off balance when the Germans mounted their Ardennes operation just three months later. He eventually decided on the broad front approach, but Montgomery as we shall see, did not come away entirely empty-handed.

The Need of a Port

By now it had become very clear that the Allies desperately needed a large working port near the front line, so as to avoid the 300-mile haul back to Normandy for replenishment. Maintaining supplies was a continual problem despite employing such innovative uses of transport as the 'Red Ball Express' which introduced a one-way loop system between St-Lô and Chartres, with every available truck running non-stop day and night. For example, from 25 to 29 August 1944, just under 6,000 trucks delivered 12,500 tons of supplies. The ideal solution would be the capture of Antwerp, so instead of going all the way with the 'narrow front' proposal, Eisenhower allowed British Second Army a major share of the hard-pressed fuel supplies at the expense of US First and Third Armies, so that they could make a swift advance on the left flank, enabling them to destroy the enemy in north-eastern France, clear the V-bomb sites in the Pas-de-Calais, capture airfields in Belgium and, most importantly, capture and open the port of Antwerp.

Week 13: 29 August–4 September 1944

Week 13 began as Week 12 had ended with more Allied progress eastwards, US VII Corps, for example, taking Soissons and crossing the Aisne. Farther east US Third Army units took Rheims and Châlons-sur-Marne. Although further progress would be made for a few more days, the grave shortage of fuel was now beginning to affect operations, as was the argument between the senior commanders, explained already, on how best to proceed with the

overall strategic battle. One can imagine General Patton's feelings, for example, when he realised that his fuel supplies would be endangered by such a plan! The debate would continue, with Eisenhower endeavouring to maintain harmony between the Allies, which inevitably resulted in his leaning more towards the British. On 30 August, 12th Army Group informed US Third Army that there would be no more fuel available until 3

Above: 'Kamerad!' This unkempt German soldier with his ad hoc white flag, was in fact a medical corpsman, one of a group picked up by passing tank column. With other medics he was trying to help some wounded comrades. (IWM - EA 4877447)

Above: Back to St-Valéry. In 1940, St-Valéry was the scene of a valiant rearguard action by the 51st Highland Division who were eventually forced to surrender. Now the tables are turned as 152 Bde of the division liberates the town. Here Maj Gen G. T. Rennie, DSO, OBE, the GOC, lights his pipe and watches his soldiers enter St-Valéry. (IWM - BU 1518)

Right: A good job done, a medic of 51st Highland Division repacks his first aid haversack before moving on. (IWM - B 8809)

Left: En route for Brussels, 3 September 1944. British tanks moving through Antoing pass under a welcoming banner. (IWM - BU 392)

Below: Same village but another banner and another Sherman. Antoing, 3 September 1944. (IWM - BU 382)

Right: Belgian troops enter Brussels. Crowds in Brussels welcome their liberators – these soldiers were especially welcome as they were Belgian. (IWM BU 579)

September. By the end of August Patton had armoured spearheads in Verdun – where they established a bridge-head across the Meuse, at Eix and St-Mihiel. His orders to his troops were to continue advancing no matter what happened – at the lowest level one tank would drain fuel from the rest of the platoon and keep the advance going. When the fuel finally ran out they would continue on foot! By 3 September, US XII Corps had consolidated its positions east of the Meuse, XV Corps were concentrated in the vicinity of Nangis, and XX Corps had secured the Verdun bridge-head and pushed patrols farther east towards Germany; far away, on the north-west coast of France, US VIII Corps was continuing its attack on the stubborn German garrison at Brest. To their north, US First Army advanced to the general line Namur–Tirlemont, taking some

25,000 prisoners in a pocket centred on the Forêt de Compiègne.

In 21st Army Group's sector, on 29 August, 11th Armd Div, reinforced by 8th Armd Bde, burst out of XXX Corps' bridge-head over the Seine on two main axes. Amiens was reached on the 31st and a bridge-head across the Somme secured. Just outside the town General Heinrich Eberbach, who had taken over command of German Seventh Army when General Paul Hausser was wounded, was captured with his Tactical HQ. The advance from XII Corps' bridge-head had begun on 30 August, their armour moving some 25 miles a day, and by midday on 1 September they had secured a crossing over the Somme at Hangest, midway between Amiens and Abbeville. The rapid advances continued; on 2 September Guards Armd Div captured Douai and Tournai,

Above: Montgomery in Louvain. Monty talks with a crowd of civilians, who surrounded his car outside the Town Hall. Louvain, some 20 miles beyond Brussels, was captured by the British in September 1944. Four years earlier when Monty had been commanding 3rd Inf Div, it had been the frontline for his division in their attempt to halt the German 'Blitzkrieg' – now the situation was very different! (IWM - B 9976)

Left: Tired infantrymen of the KSLI catch a few minutes rest by the side of a 3 RTR Sherman after another day of battle on the road to Ghent, September 1944. (Tank Museum)

Above: Maj Gen Verney, GOC 7th Armd Div, arriving at Ghent Town Hall, 8 September 1944, after its liberation by his division. (IWM - BU 771)

Below: Infantry of 95 Inf Div, US Third Army, cross a railway line below a bullet-pocked bridge support on their way towards the Moselle near Metz, 8 September 1944. The leading GI is carrying a .30 Browning machine gun. (US Army via Real War Photos - A 760)

and 11th Armd Div reached the outskirts of Lille, which they by-passed, while 7th Armd Div on the left, reached St-Pol and crossed the Béthune–Lillers road. The next targets for the fast-moving armoured columns would be: for Guards Armd – Brussels; for 11th Armd Div – Antwerp; for 7th Armd Div – Ghent. In the early hours of 3 September, Guards Armd Div crossed the Belgian frontier and by nightfall had reached the capital, its recce units fanning out around the city to control all main approaches. Strong resistance briefly delayed 11th Armd Div between Tournai and Lille, but they reach Alost that evening. Considerably more resistance was encountered on XII Corps' front, the enemy having moved two fresh divisions in to reinforce the Channel ports. Nevertheless, while 53rd Inf Div and 4th Armd Bde dealt with these formations, 7th Armd Div swung east around Lille and headed swiftly for Ghent.

On 4 September 11th Armd Div entered Antwerp and quickly disposed of the garrison save in the dock areas to the north, which took some days to clear. The docks were secured virtually intact. British Second Army had good reason to be pleased with their achievements that week. They had advanced some 250 miles in six days, the armour leading, while behind them the infantry divisions, supported by armoured brigades, had taken over the ground and mopped-up any strongpoints still holding out. The Allied front now ran from the mouth of the Somme in the north, to Troyes in the south, following the line: Lille–Brussels–Mons–Sedan–Verdun–Commercy.

Week 14: 5–11 September 1944

On 5 September a major German command change took place, FM von Rundstedt being reinstated as OB West. He was charged with holding the Allied advance while completing a new 'West Wall' on the line Albert Canal–River Meuse–Upper Moselle, a tall order given that by the time he took over the Allies already had bridge-heads across both the Albert Canal and the Meuse! This was yet again, an example, if one were needed, of Hitler's lack of up-to-date knowledge of the true situation. Von Rundstedt told his Führer that he would need at least six weeks to prepare the West Wall and asked for all available armour to reinforce his hard-pressed front-line troops. Amazingly, Hitler agreed, and although nowhere near as many tanks were available as were needed (the Allies still outnumbering them by 20 to 1), sufficient were produced to enable him to stabilise the front by mid-September.

The Allied advance had once again started in earnest with success all along the front line. In the north units of Can II Corps advanced rapidly north of the Somme; Polish Armd Div crossed the canal at St-Omer on 6 September, while nearer the coast, Can 3rd Inf Div closed up to the ports of Boulogne and Calais where it soon became clear that the enemy garrisons would not surrender without a fight. Can 2nd Inf Div, which was following up, passed through and closed on Dunkirk where a similar situation obtained. Strong detachments pushed on, reaching Nieuport and Ostend on 9 September. Canadian 4th Armd

Below: Antwerp during its liberation. A nurse of the Belgian Underground Army bandages a wounded British soldier in the front line near Antwerp docks, 11 September 1944. She was imprisoned by the Germans for 1½ years for underground activities. (IWM - BU 833)

Div then came up on the left of the Poles, securing a crossing over the Ghent–Bruges canal south-east of Bruges. Mopping-up in the town and surrounding area then took place. The Polish Armd Div then moved into the Ghent area to relieve XII Corps.

Late on 10 September British I Corps began its attack on Le Havre after a heavy bombardment from sea and air (5,000 tons of bombs were dropped in the 90 minutes before H-Hour). The defences were penetrated by 49th and 51st Inf Divs, but the port was not captured until 1145 hrs on the 12th; 12,000 prisoners were taken. It is said that Le Havre was one of the strongest fortresses on the Atlantic Wall.

British Second Army's intention was to advance with XXX Corps leading, XII Corps protecting its left flank and US First Army on its right. As a first stage in the advance on the Rhine, XXX Corps planned to get 11th Armd Div into the area Turnhout–Tilburg and Gds Armd Div into the Eindhoven area. This meant crossing numerous water obstacles,

including both the Albert Canal and the Meuse–Escaut Canal. Recce reported that all bridges were blown, but on 8 September Gds Armd crossed the Albert Canal at Beeringen and established a bridge-head there despite considerable opposition. The advance now turned north-eastwards, aimed at the De Groot bridge over the Escaut Canal near Neerpelt. By last light, 50th Inf Div had secured a small bridge-head over the canal to the SW of Gheel. After gradually extending the bridge-heads, Gds Armd broke through, then reached and captured the De Groot bridge on the 10th, extending the bridge-head the following day. The effects of the arrival of German reinforcements was now being felt, with the enemy, as Montgomery puts it: '... developing more spirit against our bridge-heads over the Escaut Canal, and had clearly received reinforcements of better calibre,'

South of British Second Army, Hodge's US First Army pushed towards Liège with US VII Corps and crossed the Meuse at Sedan. On 11 September patrols crossed the German border

Below: GIs moving through the rubble of Pontfarcy in the Brest peninsula. They pass close by a KOed enemy tank – a PzKpfw IV Ausf H. More of this model were produced than any other Mk IV. (US Army via Real War Photos - A 3161)

near Aachen, creating panic among the civilians, but the action was not followed up.

Patton's US Third Army lost VII Corps which was transferred to US Ninth Army (General Simpson) which was now preparing for action, but 83rd Inf and 6th Armd Divs were transferred to XV Corps, thus remaining as 'Georgie's Boys'. XX Corps was ordered to seize Metz, advance east of the Moselle, seize Mainz and secure a bridge-head across the Rhine. XII Corps was to seize Nancy and secure a bridge-head over the Moselle, protecting the southern flank until relieved by XV Corps. They were also told to be ready to move swiftly to take Mannheim and seize a Rhine bridge-head. Fuel supplies continued to improve (on 7 September, for the first time in several days, more fuel was available than was required!), but a new crisis loomed – a severe shortage of artillery ammunition, but this was fortunately alleviated by the end of the week for all calibres except 105mm howitzer.

Week 15: 12–18 September 1944
(See Chapter 6 for Operation 'Market Garden' – the Arnhem operation which began on 17 September and ended on 26 September.)

In mid-September Can First Army was commanding British I Corps, which was relieving British XII Corps in the Antwerp area, and Can II Corps which was operating in the coastal belt. The intention was for British I Corps to advance north across the Antwerp–Turnhout Canal, while Can II Corps cleared the area to the west of the port and up to the southern shores of the Scheldt estuary. At the same time the Canadians invested Dunkirk and stormed the garrisons of Boulogne and Calais. Within these three ports were some 30,000 troops who had been left behind to hold them as fortresses. Boulogne had a garrison of more than 9,000 men, with extremely strong defences along the high ground which formed a crescent around the port; the main features had been made into individual strongpoints, with concrete bunkers, wire and minefields. The assault was delayed by bad weather and this meant that some 8,000 civilians could be evacuated before Can 3rd Inf Div launched its attack, on 17 September, with two brigades, heavily supported by artillery and from the air. It took six days to capture all the isolated strongpoints. Coastal artillery in England helped in the assault – on 17 September the

Below: Trucks of the US First Army crossing the Albert Canal via a pontoon treadway bridge near Maastricht, 12 September 1944. (Tank Museum)

Above: Closing in on Brest. Troops of US Third Army set up their 57mm M1 anti-tank gun on the outskirts of Recovrance, on the way to Brest, the second largest naval port in France. The M1 was a copy of the British 6pdr anti-tank gun. (IWM - EA 38584)

Right: Dramatic picture of an M18 Hellcat firing its 76mm gun at point-blank range into a pillbox, during street fighting in Brest. The Hellcat was normally a tank destroyer; however, its armour-piercing ammuntion no doubt made a hell of a mess of the pillbox! (IWM EA 37636)

Left: Men of 141st Inf Regt, 36th Inf Div, US Seventh Army, slog through the rain into Luxeuil, 17 September 1944. (US Army via Real War Photos - A 3203)

Below: GIs of F Company, 2nd Bn 141st Inf Regt, 36th Inf Div, ride on the back of a tank and a half-track towards their objective near Soultz, 18 September 1944. Note the Browning .50 cal heavy machine gun on a skate-ring mount and the attentive gunner watching the skies (is he – like Rommel – wearing British anti-gas goggles?). (US Army via Real War

South Foreland Battery near Dover scored a direct hit on a battery near Calais, at a remarkable range of 42,000 yards!

On the 12th the German garrison of Le Havre surrendered as has been mentioned. On the 15th British Second Army secured a second crossing-point over the Meuse–Escaut Canal. To the south, more units of US First Army reached the German border between Aachen and Trier on the 12th, and took Maastricht and Eisden on the 15th. In US Third Army's area, both XII and XX Corps were fighting to maintain their bridge-heads over the Moselle, with XII Corps enlarging and expanding theirs north and south of Nancy, while XX Corps on their left, pushed infantry across north of Bayon. In the south XV Corps' infantry reached Neufchâteau, Mirecourt and Charmes. There were still some fuel shortages, but with PLUTO reaching Chartres these would soon be obviated. XV Corps continued to push eastwards, 79th Inf Div reaching Ramecourt on the 14th, while French 2nd Armd Div took Mattaincourt and made contact with elements

of US Seventh Army advancing from the Mediterranean. There were heavy enemy counter-attacks against 80th Inf Div's bridge-head over the Moselle, but they were dealt with on the 15th. On the 17th XV Corps was ordered to take Mannheim and secure a bridge-head over the Rhine. On the same day XX Corps launched a co-ordinated attack on the heavily fortified city of Metz, with 5th Inf Div assaulting from the south and 90th Inf Div from the west. XV Corps' attack began on the 18th, 79th Inf Div crossing the Moselle near Bayon and advancing to Gerbéviller.

Week 16: 19–25 September 1944

On the 19th back in Brittany, the German garrison of Brest finally surrendered to US VII Corps' 8th Inf Div. Taken prisoner with 12,000 others was the redoubtable paratroop commander Major General Hermann Ramcke, who had famously commanded the Ramcke Para Bde in North Africa. Hitler had ordered that the Diamonds to his Knight's Cross be parachuted into the beleaguered port. In 21st

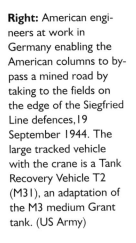

Right: American engineers at work in Germany enabling the American columns to by-pass a mined road by taking to the fields on the edge of the Siegfried Line defences, 19 September 1944. The large tracked vehicle with the crane is a Tank Recovery Vehicle T2 (M31), an adaptation of the M3 medium Grant tank. (US Army)

Army Group's area, to the west of XXX Corps' advance towards Arnhem (see Chapter 6), Canadian units crossed the Escaut Canal and began their offensive to clear the north bank of the Scheldt estuary so as to open up the vital port of Antwerp to the sea. General Eisenhower had given top priority to these operations. On the 22nd, also in Can First Army's sector, Boulogne surrendered to Can II Corps'

3rd Inf Div (9,535 prisoners), while by the 24th Can I Corps' 2nd Inf Div had established a bridge-head over the Antwerp–Turnhout canal. On the 25th, 3rd Inf Div attacked the defences of Calais after an intensive artillery bombardment. The enemy positions here were similar to those at Le Havre and Boulogne, and there were additional batteries at Cap Gris-Nez and Sangatte.

Above: A section of men of the King's Own Scottish Borderers of 3rd Inf Div move on to new territory on 19 September 1944 – they are clearly expecting to do some digging in. (IWM - B 10120)

Left: Brest captured. Some 35,000 enemy surrendered in Brest on 20 September 1944. This group, waiting to be taken off for interrogation and POW camp, includes both Army (*Heer*) and Navy (*Kriegsmarine*) officers. 23 September 1944. (IWM - KY 483596)

Above right: Always one more river to cross! First vehicles over this newly constructed bridge across the River Vire belonged to 35th Inf Div of US Third Army. (US Army via Real War Photos - A 3162)

Below: A good initiative by Shermans of the US 8th Tank Battalion, 4th Armored Division, finding a crossing over the silted-up, but still very muddy and treacherous, National Canal near Bayon, 20 September 1944. (US Army)

In US Third Army's sector XX Corps continued to pound Metz but made little progress. On the 24th leading patrols were probing the outer defences of the Siegfried Line, but were met with strong resistance from pillboxes and other fortifications. There was extensive flooding in all sectors other than to the west of the city.

Week 17: 26 September–2 October 1944

US First Army began a new offensive against the Siegfried Line between Aachen and Geilenkirchen to the north.

In US Third Army's sector the assault on Metz continued all week, heavy artillery fire being directed on the forts (two casements and an ammunition dump were blown up in Fort Jeanne d'Arc but it did not fall). On the 27th XX Corps put in a major attack on Fort Driant but was forced to withdraw. At the end of the week, on 2 October, XX Corps, supported by XIX Tactical Air Command, launched a heavy ground and air attack on Fort Driant on the west bank of the Moselle, but still encountered heavy resistance when they entered the fort next day. Heavy fire was also directed on Forts

Jeanne d'Arc and Verdun, also Batteries Moselle and Marivall, but despite continual bombardment, they all held out. Fuel rationing had to be re-instituted as supplies were down to 50 per cent, which hampered all Third Army's advances.

The Canadians had more success with the capture of the Channel ports, the citadel at Calais falling on the 28th and the town being entered on the same day. An armistice was then granted to allow for the evacuation of civilians, the attack not resuming until midday on the 30th. By last light all organised opposition had ceased, some 10,000 prisoners having been taken during the attacks. This would be the last

of the 'fortress' ports to be cleared, Dunkirk would merely be 'bottled up' and would remain so for the remainder of the war, becoming the last French town to be liberated. The responsibility for Dunkirk would be handed over to the Czech Independent Armoured Brigade, thus leaving the Canadians free to concentrate on clearing the Scheldt which Montgomery ordered General Crerar to accomplish '... with all possible speed'. An account of this operation is given in a later chapter.

Above left: Crossing the Moselle River, 20 September 1944. Infantry plus a jeep with a trailer laden with ammunition boxes, crossing a pontoon bridge over the river. (US Army)

Week 18: 3–9 October 1944

British Second Army operations towards the end of September were designed to widen and

Left: A Sherman belonging to 3 RTR of 11th Armd Div moves up to the frontline, 26 September 1944. The signs on the front of the Sherman are: '52' – unit serial number, the three armd regts in the armd bde were numbered 51, 52 and 53; the 'triangle' with a '3' inside shows it belongs to 3 Tp of 'A' Sqn; the running bull (black on a yellow background) was the divisional sign of 11th Armd Div. (Tank Museum)

Above: US Third Army engineers completing a pontoon bridge across the Moselle. The Model C66 mobile crane which is lifting one of the pontoons could lift up to 5,500lb on its full 25ft extension and 13,000lb on its shorter 10ft radius. (IWM - EA 58281)

Above right: Troops of US Third Army wading across a stream in the Moselle River valley, whilst a medical jeep, carrying stretcher cases, makes its way back to the other bank. (IWM - EA 38139)

strengthen the Nijmegen salient, in preparation for the coming battle of the Rhineland, which Montgomery hoped to start on about 10 October. He therefore issued instructions to regroup, but towards the end of the first week of October it became very clear that any such assault would have to be delayed in view of other commitments. The strength of counter-attacks around the Nijmegen bridge-head area showed the need for considerable reinforcement there, to make certain it was held. On the First Canadian Army Front there was considerable stiffening of enemy resistance – it was estimated, for example, that there were some 20 enemy divisions/strong battlegroups, including four panzer divisions in the area from Roermond to Breskens. In addition, the nature of the country, criss-crossed by water obstacles, favoured the defence, so Montgomery reluctantly had to postpone his offensive and concentrate on Can First Army's endeavour to clear the Scheldt, while British Second Army dealt with the enemy bridge-head west of the Meuse.

US First Army continued its attacks north of Aachen and had some success in breaking through the Siegfried Line in some areas.

In US Third Army's sector Metz was still being pounded, but it was clear that the enemy was determined to hold out as long as possible. Elsewhere, Patton's troops had more success, XII Corps enlarging their bridge-head by attacking to the north-east, capturing

Fossieux (35th Inf Div), Moivrons (6th Armd Div) and Lixières (80th Inf Div).

Week 19: 10–16 October 1944

In British Second Army's sector, VIII Corps had been ordered to assault from Boxmeer towards Venraij, with US 7th Armd Div (under command) making an attack from Deurne. Then 11th Armd Div would pass through and make for Venlo, while another attack would be made towards the Maas, to capture Roermond. This operation was planned to start on 12 October, and, despite dogged resistance, Venraij was taken on the 17th, but operations were then concluded for a time.

In US First Army's sector, attacks around Aachen continued to make ground; the city's garrison commander declined an invitation to surrender and house-to-house fighting continued amid the ruins.

On US Third Army's front, 6th Armd Div cleared Chenicourt and pushed on to Aulnois-sur-Seine. At Metz, Task Force Warnock (Brigadier Alva C. Warnock), took over from Task Force Driant and assaults continued on the tunnels and forts, but without success. On 9–10 October 90th Inf Div was engaged in fierce house-to-house fighting in Maizières-lès-Metz. During this week 12th Army Group drastically reduced the issue of field artillery ammunition by 95 per cent (from 12 October to 7 November), so that the troops had to make do with tanks, TDs, AA guns and even

captured enemy weapons. Considerable enemy troop movements were noted in XII Corps' area, and heavy rail and road movement was also observed in XX Corps sector. US Third Army was virtually on the defensive as required by 12th Army Group. Bad weather put a stop to air activity, and lack of fuel prevented ground movement (Third Army asked for 330,000 gallons plus of POL on 16 October – and received none!).

In the far south, in General Devers' 6th Army Group, French First Army's 3rd Algerian Div reached Cornimont by the end of the week, then, accompanied by French 1st Armd Div, launched an attack in the Vosges. In US Seventh Army's sector, VI Corps units began to move from the north-west southwards, towards Bruyères, but were heavily engaged when they reached there.

Summary. Enemy resistance was clearly hardening everywhere and the Allies had much to do to consolidate their current positions – in the Scheldt estuary and at Metz for example – so by mid-October the Allied drive to the Rhine had virtually come to a halt. The British and Canadians were fully occupied in the north; in the central sectors US First and Third Armies were fighting hard along the Siegfried Line from Aachen down to Trier and southwards into the area of the southern Moselle. To their south, US 6th Army Group was now deployed on the right of US 12th Army Group, so that the area of operations continued right down to the Swiss frontier. At a conference in Brussels on 18 October, Eisenhower reiterated his plans: 21st Army Group must concentrate on the opening up of Antwerp. British Second Army was then to advance south-eastwards between the Meuse and the Rhine, on or about 10 November, in support of US First Army which would attempt to cross the Rhine in the Cologne area (planned for 1–5 November). Their right flank would be protected by US Ninth Army, which would then advance and assist in capturing the Ruhr.

Above: Gen Manton Eddy, CG XII Corps, uses the bonnet of a Jeep as a map table, whilst he briefs three of his commanders. Left to right they are: Brig Gen Holmes Dager (Cdr CCB), Maj Gen Willard S. Paul (CG 26 Inf Div), Maj Gen 'Tiger Jack' Wood (CG 4th Armd Div), Maj Gen Manton Eddy, and an unidentified colonel of 4th Armd. (US Army via Patton Museum)

Taking a Gamble

Despite Montgomery's determination to finish the war as quickly as possible and hence his support for the narrow front approach, he was still basically a cautious commander, not given to rash decisions, preferring to have 'belt and braces' – as his refusal to attack Rommel in North Africa until his forces were completely ready, clearly indicated. So his Arnhem gamble was totally uncharacteristic. Yet it was an extremely bold stroke which, had it succeeded, would undoubtedly have considerably shortened the war.

Having liberated Belgium, Montgomery's 21st Army Group now faced no fewer than five water obstacles which could be crossed at: the Neder Rijn at Arnhem, the Waal at Nijmegen, the Maas at Grave and the two main transverse canals running between Grave and British Second Army's bridge-heads over the Escaut Canal (the Wilhelmina Canal, north of Eind-

hoven; the Zuid Willemsvaart which ran parallel to the River Maas, linking the towns of Helmond and 's Hertogenbosch). There were road and railway bridges at both Arnhem and Nijmegen and a road bridge at Grave, all of which were still intact. The plan was to lay a corridor of airborne troops (three airborne divisions – two US and one British, plus the Polish Parachute Brigade, all flown out from England) across the waterways, taking the bridges at Veghel, Grave, Nijmegen and Arnhem; then for British Second Army to advance along the corridor, with General Horrocks' XXX Corps leading.

The Detailed Plan

Airborne troops. Allocation of I Airborne Corps' targets was as follows.

Arnhem bridge:

    1 British Ab Div, with Polish Para Bde under command (52 Airportable Div was to be

Below: US 101st Airborne Division. Their objectives were the bridges and defiles on the British XXX Corps axis between Grave and Eindhoven. They were soon established at Son and secured the Veghel bridge intact. The photograph shows men of the 101st just after landing as they disperse to their objectives. The jeep was brought in by glider. (US Army via Real War Photos - A 376B)

flown in north of Arnhem as soon as airstrips could be made available, to strengthen the bridge-head)

Nijmegen and Grave bridges, plus high ground between Goesbeek and Nijmegen:

US 82nd Ab Div

The bridges and defiles on British XXX Corps' axis between Grave and Eindhoven:

US 101st Ab Div

It would be impossible to fly in the entire Airborne Corps in one lift, because there weren't enough transport aircraft; in fact it would take four days to fly in everything that was required. The air lift programme was scheduled as:

Day 1: 17 September
US 82nd and 101st Ab Divs would each drop three parachute Regimental Combat Teams (RCTs)

British 1st Ab Div would drop a para bde, and land two-thirds of the air-landing brigade

Day 2:
Further elements of US 82nd and 101st Ab Divs and remainder of Br 1st Ab Div

Day 3:
Remainder of US 82nd and 101st Ab Divs
Polish Para Bde

Ground troops. The intention was that British XXX Corps' advance would be co-ordinated with the airborne drops so as to gain maximum surprise and dislocation. They would thrust northwards as fast as possible from the Meuse–Escaut Canal bridge-head along the airborne corridor to secure the area Arnhem–Nunspeet, the advance being spear-headed by Gds Armd Div, whilst 43rd and 50th Inf Divs followed up. Should any of the bridges be destroyed the armour was to fan out

Above: US 101st Airborne Division. Part of the crew of a glider pose beside their craft before take-off from an aerodrome in UK. There were various models of the Waco glider; for example, the CG 4A could carry 15 fully armed and equipped men; the CG 10A double that number; whilst the 13A could manage a jeep and gun crew or 30 men. (US Army via Real War Photos - A 376A)

Above: US 82nd Airborne Division. Their objectives were the bridges at Nijmegen and Grave. Here some glider-borne troops orientate themselves before moving off from the landing zone. (IWM - EA 37782).

along the river bank and, assisted by the airborne troops, cover bridging operations which were to be carried out by 43rd Inf Div. This division was also given the ultimate task of securing the area from Apeldoorn south to points of contact with 1st Ab Div and to secure crossings over the River Ijssel at Deventer and Zutphen. The Corps reserve would consist of 50th Inf Div which would ultimately occupy the high ground north of Arnhem, pushing elements eastwards to secure a crossing over the Ijssel at Doesburg. The task of opening the main road axis to the north was allotted to the two US Ab Divs; 8th Armd Bde would join 101st Ab Div and assist in holding the corridor through Eindhoven, Veghel and Grave.

The Battle: 17–26 September 1944

The morning of the 17th dawned fair and generally favourable for airborne operations. The aircraft converged on the dropping and landing zones at 1300 hrs as planned. Surprise was generally achieved and enemy opposition was light. Paratroops of US 101st Ab Div were soon established at Son, between Eindhoven and St-Oedenrode. They secured the bridge at Veghel intact, but that over the Wilhelmina Canal was blown as they approached. US 82nd Ab Div also landed according to plan, seized the bridge over the Maas at Grave intact and, later, secured the two bridges over the Maas–Waal Canal between Grave and Nijmegen. They failed to rush the Nijmegen bridge but reported that it was still intact. Their main problem was contacting British 1st Ab Div at Arnhem who, it seemed, were holding the northern end of the bridge, and air recce showed that gliders had landed in its vicinity.

British XXX Corps ordered Gds Armd Div to begin their advance at 1425 hrs. It was covered by a rolling barrage and moved astride the Eindhoven road, in conjunction with a 'cab rank' of rocket-firing Typhoons on call. However, strong opposition was encountered almost immediately and only some six miles was achieved on the first day. It soon became

Left: The Nijmegen bridge was not captured until 20 September, then by a joint attack by US paratroopers and XXX Corps. Here, one of the wounded German defenders awaits medical attention on the bridge roadway. (IWM - 38567)

Below: Allied tanks roll across the newly captured Nijmegen bridge, on their way towards 'the bridge too far' at Arnhem. (IWM - EA 44531)

Right: Maj Gen Matthew Bunker Ridgway, then CG of XVIII Airborne Corps, talking with Maj Gen Jones H. Canin, CG 82nd Ab Div. It is easy to see why Ridgway was known as 'Old Iron Tits'! (US Army via Real War Photos AB 2013)

clear that more infantry were needed, so a brigade from 50th Inf Div was brought forward and the advance continued at first light on the 18th. The armoured spearhead brushed aside enemy opposition at Aalst, but could not break into Eindhoven, which was strongly defended. The tanks then tried to bypass to the east, but were again held up by strong enemy positions. The bridges to the west of the town were not strong enough to take tanks, but armoured cars did get across and made contact with 101st Ab Div to the north-west of Eindhoven, who reported that the Son bridge had been blown. The assault on the town continued from all sides and eventually, at about 1700 hrs, the Guards broke through. Bridging work at Son was immediately put in hand, while 50th Inf Div mopped-up and secured the De Groot bridge. After an enemy counter-attack had been held, the responsibility for this bridge-head was transferred to VIII Corps who took over command of 50th Inf Div.

To the north of Eindhoven, US 101st Ab Div strengthened its grip on the vital points along the axis all the way up to the Grave bridge, while 82nd Ab Div continued its unsuccessful attempt to reach the Nijmegen bridge. At about this time the enemy launched the first of a series of counter-attacks from the direction of the Reichswald Forest, which initially reached one of the landing zones before being repulsed. While this was taking place, a glider lift of reinforcements landed, having been delayed some four hours by bad weather. News from Arnhem was still scarce. The main body of airborne troops was established west of the town, and elements of the para bde were holding out at the road bridge which was apparently still intact. But the enemy was holding Arnhem town in strength with tanks and SP guns. The reinforcements which had arrived late now found themselves surrounded and held up at the western end of town. By last light the situation had not improved, 1st Ab

Div being split in three locations and running short of supplies; re-supply had failed because of bad weather and heavy enemy AA.

Elements of Gds Armd Div crossed the Son bridge at 0615 hrs on the 19th and less than three hours later had advanced some 25 miles to link up with 82nd Ab Div at the Grave bridge. Farther north, the bridge over the Maas–Waal Canal was found to be unsuitable for tanks and a detour had to be found – via a crossing just north of Heumen. Leading armoured cars reached the banks of the Waal by early afternoon, while the forward armoured brigade was concentrated some three miles south of Nijmegen. Heavy counter-attacks delayed the assault on the Nijmegen bridge; the town was entered at about 1845 hrs, but the bridge could not be reached and the attack had to be called off. At Arnhem the situation was now becoming critical. Only

troops of the parachute brigade were at the bridge, holding a small area in its immediate vicinity, while the rest of the division was trying to concentrate some four miles to the west. Enemy tanks and artillery were reducing the buildings to rubble, food and ammunition was running out. In 101st Ab Div's area, fighting had been heavy all day, a series of counter-attacks being launched against the Eindhoven–Nijmegen section of the axis. It was later discovered that these attacks were put in by 107th Panzer Brigade which had arrived 'unexpectedly', and undetected, in the area. They mounted a strong attack on the Son bridge, but were beaten off. The weather was bad all day, which seriously dislocated the air-lift programme, affecting both reinforcement and re-supply. It also meant that air to ground support was limited, and enemy movement could not be prevented, especially around the

Above: British 1st Airborne Division. Their objective was the Arnhem bridge, the farthest north of the 1st Allied Airborne Army's airborne corridor. Here, four-engined Stirlings of the RAF drop supplies to the airborne troops. Unfortunately most supplies landed in enemy hands, whilst many aircraft were damaged or lost. (IWM - BU 1092)

Arnhem bridge-head. Those transport aircraft which did manage to fly, dropped their loads on DZs which were now in enemy hands, because faulty communications had prevented them being altered. It was a similar dismal picture in both other divisional areas: 101st Ab Div receiving only 66 per cent of its requirements, 82nd Ab Div just 25 per cent. Most importantly, bad weather had prevented the Polish Para Bde from taking off from England; they were to have been dropped south of Arnhem to reinforce the beleaguered 1st Ab Div, so the situation was critical.

And it now began to go from bad to worse. Enemy fire, especially AA, increased, so that any aircraft that managed to get to the DZs and LZs came under very heavy fire. Access to the main Eindhoven road was becoming hopelessly congested and efforts to widen the corridor met with stiff resistance. Progress on both flanks was described as being 'depressingly slow', the nature of the terrain, which was criss-crossed with waterways, made wider movement extremely difficult, and the 'corridor' was extremely vulnerable to enemy attack. Three major tasks now faced the Allies: to capture the Nijmegen bridge as quickly as possible; to strengthen 82nd Ab Div because the enemy was building up forces in the Reichswald Forest area; to relieve the hard-pressed

1st Ab Div at Arnhem. During the morning of 20 September, combined US/British forces cleared Nijmegen up to the southern approaches to the bridge. In the town the defenders had been reinforced and bitter fighting ensued. That afternoon, following some swift instruction on the use of British assault boats, men of 504 RCT began to row across the Waal, in full view of the enemy and with only sufficient boats to carry one battalion at a time. On the northern bank, the ground was extremely open and flat, fire support was limited, and the smoke-screen laid down to cover the operation proved ineffective. Ignoring all these problems, the US paratroopers carried out a magnificent operation. Despite heavy casualties, they had captured the northern end of the bridge by 1845 hrs and, coupled with a head-on attack by Gds Armd Div's tanks on the southern end, the bridge was taken, the demolition charges removed and the last defenders eliminated. While 43rd Inf Div was closing up from the south, plans were made to resume the advance the following day.

In the Arnhem area, however, the situation had become desperate. It had still proved impossible to bring in the Poles, so the link-up between Nijmegen and Arnhem had not been made, and more and more enemy forces were

Below: British paratroopers moving forward towards Arnhem from their DZ, carrying much of their kit and ammunition in lightweight, two-wheel trailers. (IWM - BU 1090)

concentrating around 1st Ab Div which had now withdrawn to a small perimeter around the Heveadrop ferry and the Oosterbeek woods. Hemmed in on every side, they were being subjected to concentrated artillery and mortar fire. Arnhem town was now completely in enemy hands and nothing was known of the fate of the survivors of the para bde. In the southern sector, the 101st still held its positions in the face of continued attacks against the corridor. The enemy did reach the main road at one point near Son, but were driven off by an armoured counter-attack which had restored the situation by midday. Little progress was made on either flank.

From 21 September onwards all efforts were concentrated on relieving the Arnhem bridgehead forces. The weather, except on the 23rd, remained very difficult for flying, and ground movement was equally slow. The Gds Armd Div spearhead resumed operations in an attempt to get northwards, but was halted by a strong anti-tank-gun screen, south of Bessem. It was well-nigh impossible for tanks to get off the roads which generally ran on banks some six feet above the fields, with deep drainage ditches on both sides. On the 21st, two-thirds of the Polish Para Bde was dropped N and NW

of Elst, between Arnhem and Nijmegen. They sustained many casualties in Elst, which delayed them in their main task which was to get across the Neder Rijn and reinforce the British paratroops who were now cut off from the river because the Germans had captured the Heveadrop ferry terminal.

On the 22nd, 43rd Inf Div resumed the attack northwards from the Nijmegen bridgehead, but were held up at Elst. However, a mixed force of tanks and infantry did manage to detour to the west and join up with the Poles at Driel; together they reached the Neder Rijn. Under close, concentrated fire they tried to get supplies across, but the amphibious trucks were unable to negotiate the steep banks, so very few stores got across that night. Further south, between Uden and Veghel, there was more trouble, strong panzer and panzergrenadier forces temporarily cutting XXX Corps' axis. By the afternoon of the 23rd the road had been re-opened and the remainder of Polish Para Bde, plus 82nd Ab Div's Glider Regt, were flown in and some 250 Polish troops were ferried across the Neder Rijn that night to reinforce 1st Ab Div. Next night infantry detachments crossed the river but failed to make contact with the paras. At

Left: OC 'C' Coy of 5th Border Regt, Maj 'Jock' Neill, seen here in a slit trench with his machine gun officer, Lt McCartney, had been wounded twice in both arms and legs when this photograph was taken on the 20th, but continued fighting. (IWM - BU 1102)

Right: The Hartenstein Hotel, 23 September 1944. Troops take advantage of a lull in the fighting to clean their weapons and brew up. In the background are the tennis courts where the German prisoners were kept. (IWM - BU 1114)

Below: One of the two-man slits in the shrinking airborne perimeter. (IWM - BU 111)

first light, intense fire from the high ground overlooking the river put a stop to these operations. To the south, heavy fighting flared up again in and around Elst and Bemmel, and during the afternoon of 24 September the main axis was again cut south of Veghel. Fighting continued and the axis was not re-opened until the 26th.

On the night of 25 September Field Marshal Montgomery reluctantly decided to withdraw the Arnhem bridge-head. The troops had suffered grievous casualties and were short of ammunition and supplies; their situation was no longer tenable. In all about 2,200 survivors managed to escape, leaving some 7,000 killed, wounded or captured. Montgomery later wrote: 'We had undertaken a difficult operation, attended by considerable risks. It was justified because, had good weather obtained, there was no doubt that we should have attained full success. The battle of Arnhem was ninety per cent successful. We were left in possession of crossings over four major water obstacles including the Maas and the Waal.'

7
Clearing the Scheldt

Opening-up Antwerp

The capture of Antwerp on 4 September 1944 with its port facilities in good condition, did not solve the Allies' supply problems because the enemy still held the Scheldt estuary in strength and could thus prevent shipping from using the port. General Eisenhower considered the opening of Antwerp to be of vital importance prior to the conquest of Germany and on 22 September gave absolute priority to operations to liberate the area. The task was passed to the Can First Army by Field Marshal Montgomery a few days later as their primary target which had to be achieved as quickly as possible. Although in scale it was a small operation by comparison with others, such as the breakout from Normandy, or the battle for France, or even the Arnhem operation, it was of vital importance and deserves to be looked at in isolation. Indeed, Mont-

gomery wrote later: 'It had become necessary to devote the whole of our resources into getting Antwerp working at once, and I had to shut down all other offensive operations in 21st Army Group until this object was achieved.'[1]

This did not mean however that the German garrison in the remaining stubborn 'fortress' of Dunkirk would be let off the hook. Instead, as already mentioned, while the Canadians concentrated on clearing the Scheldt, responsibility for the siege of Dunkirk was passed to the Czech Independent Armoured Brigade Group, commanded by Major-General Alois Lishka. For part of this siege the Churchills of 7th RTR would also be under command of the Czechs. Dunkirk would remain 'bottled up' for the remainder of the war, being the last French town to be liberated – on 10 May 1945.

Left: Whilst the Canadians concentrated on clearing the Scheldt, the stubborn garrison in Dunkirk had to be 'bottled up'. This was done by the Czech Indep Armd Bde, which had both French and British troops under command. Here sappers of the bde patrol the flooded areas around Dunkirk from their base at Bulscamp near Furnes. (IWM - B 15132)

Right: French infantry were also holding the line around Dunkirk, along the De La Clome near Bercues. This team man a captured German MG 42 machine gun – one of the best MGs of WW2. Its high rate of fire made a noise likened to tearing linoleum! (IWM - B 15116)

Operations in the Scheldt estuary were not made any easier by the fact that much of the area consisted of reclaimed land – flat, muddy and in some places flooded, a truly horrible place in which to have to fight. But, as on D-Day, the Allies had a number of 'aces' up their sleeves, two important ones being the Royal Naval Support Squadron, which would provide close fire support for the required amphibious operations, and yet more of the remarkable 'Funnies', the strange AFVs of 79th Armd Div. These factors, combined with the bravery of the Canadian and British troops and their sea and air cover, meant that victory was assured, though not without a difficult campaign which lasted from 2 October until 8 November, by which time the minesweepers were already clearing the river ahead of the first convoy which reached the port on the 26th.

The Plan

The clearing of the Scheldt estuary involved the capture of three separate yet related areas: the coastal plain between Ternuezen and Knokke (known locally as 'Breskens Island') where German heavy coastal batteries at Breskens and Cadzand covered the approaches to the estuary; the isthmus and peninsula of South Beveland, which stuck out into the Scheldt; finally, Walcheren Island, where some 25 heavy batteries covered shipping in the estuary. The area was garrisoned by tough, seasoned troops who had fought on the Eastern Front – the mainland south of the estuary was held by German 64th Inf Div which had been left isolated when Fifteenth Army had withdrawn eastwards. Walcheren was garrisoned by German 70th Inf Div, known curiously as the 'Whitebread Division' because most of its 7½ thousand troops had stomach problems and required special diets – though this would not affect their fighting ability! On South Beveland were elements of a divisional battlegroup, and between the estuary and Turnhout were troops from German 346th, 711th and 719th Inf Divs.

The Allies planned to clear the estuary in three phases:-

1. Clear 'Breskens Island', while at the same

time sealing off the South Beveland peninsula by a thrust from Antwerp.

2. Clear South Beveland by advancing along the isthmus in conjunction with an amphibious assault across the estuary from the south.

3. Capture Walcheren by a series of concentric assaults from east, south and west (which would entail a second crossing of the estuary to take Flushing), together with a seaborne assault by a force coming from one the Channel ports.

Execution

Phase 1. On 1 October, Can 2nd Inf Div crossed the Antwerp–Turnhout canal and advanced westwards towards the northern suburbs of Antwerp. Resistance was scattered and by the evening of 4 October the Canadians had cleared the Merxem–Eekeren area and their leading troops had reached Putte, about halfway to the peninsula. They continued to make steady progress, but as they

approached Korteven, resistance increased and they were unable to capture the village. The enemy launched numerous counter-attacks, but on 16 October the village of Woensdrecht was occupied. Meanwhile on the right flank of Can First Army, I Corps advanced on the line of the Antwerp–Turnhout canal. The Polish Armd Div crossed the Dutch frontier north of Merksplas on 1 October, 49th Inf Div at this time being engaged in fighting north of St. Lenaarts. By 5 October leading troops were in Alphen, and about four miles from Tilburg, and were able to hold their positions despite continual counter-attacks over the next few days. In the third week of October, Can 4th Armd Div was switched from the Leopold Canal sector to join I Corps, and US 104th Inf Div was also moved into the sector. From 20 October good progress was made northwards so that by the evening of the 23rd, Can 4th Armd Div had crossed the Dutch frontier near Essen and was swinging westwards towards Bergen-op-Zoom. This manoeuvre, together

Above: The new amphibian – to the British Army that was – to be used in considerable numbers whilst clearing the Scheldt was the American 'Buffalo' Landing Vehicle Tracked – two main versions of which were used by 79th Armd Div, the LVT 2 and the LVT 4, the latter having a hinged stern ramp which meant that the engine had to be repositioned. This Buffalo, belonging to 11 RTR, was manoeuvring off Beveland, just before the assault took place there on 30 October 1944. (IWM HU 71712)

Above: Buffaloes of 5 ARRE, 79th Armd Div, are loaded onto LCTs at Ostend for the Westkapelle operation. There were 102 Buffaloes manned by 5 ARRE and 11 RTR in the assault, together with 2 Sherman gun tanks and 10 Flails from 1st Lothians, plus other 'Funnies'. (Author's Collection)

with continued pressure at Woensdrecht, successfully sealed off the South Beveland peninsula and opened the way for an advance along the isthmus.

In the Leopold Canal area south of 'Breskens Island', Can 3rd Inf Div planned an assault across the canal, due north from Maldegem, while a brigade-sized amphibious landing would take place on the NE corner of the 'island'. Enemy positions on the north bank of the Leopold Canal were extremely difficult to dislodge because they were on the reverse slope of the canal dike, so it was decided to use the Churchill Crocodile flame-throwers of 141st Regiment RAC against them prior to the assault. H-Hour was in the early hours of 6 October and the attacking companies launched their assault boats as soon as the flaming had stopped. On the right all went well, but on the left there were heavy casualties from machine-gun fire. However, the attackers managed to gain a foothold on the far bank and to hold it all that day despite

counter-attacks and continuous mortaring. On the 7th, reinforcements were ferried across, but it was still touch-and-go until a Bailey bridge had been completed four days later. The amphibious force landed at about 0200 hrs on 8 October, with minimum opposition and maximum surprise. But at daybreak the battery at Flushing (Vlissingen) and the guns in the Biervliet area began to bombard the beach and the approaches. But by 0500 hrs the Buffaloes[2] used by the assault force had returned to embark the follow-up echelon which began to arrive at about 0900 hrs. Resistance intensified as the day progressed, but the advance continued westwards along the coast, while other elements pushed inland. By last light the beach-head was 2–3 miles deep. Because opposition had been so strong on the Leopold Canal, it was decided to reinforce the beach-head and push down southwards along the western bank of the Savojaards Plaat inlet, so as to open an inland route via the village of Isabella; this was achieved by last light on 14

October. The 52nd Lowland Inf Div was now arriving in the theatre under command of Can First Army, and took over the Leopold Canal bridge-head. The additional troops, plus excellent air support soon quickened the pace of operations, Breskens being captured on the 22nd. More than half the 'island' was now in British/Canadian hands; the remainder was left to Can 3rd Inf Div, while 52nd Lowland prepared to cross the Scheldt estuary.

Phase 2. Early on 24 October Can 2nd Inf Div began its advance along the Beveland isthmus, leading to the peninsula, their progress slowed by the difficult going. There was considerable flooding, especially on the approaches to the Beveland Canal, and all unflooded roads were cratered and mined. Slowly the Canadians forced their way to the west, sometimes waist-deep in water. By 25 October they had reached Rilland and the following day were only six miles from the Beveland Canal. Meanwhile, on the night of 25/26 October a brigade of the Lowland Div sailed from Terneuzen in Buffaloes and LCAs to make an assault landing near Baarland. On the left-hand beach the landing was unopposed, but on the right there was some shelling. A squadron of DD Sherman amphibious tanks of the Staffordshire Yeomanry had got across the estuary without difficulty but were then stopped by mudflats and dikes. Despite counter-attacks, the beach-head was being extended beyond Oudelande in the west. On 27–28 October, while this was being done, leading troops of Can 2nd Inf Div reached the Beveland Canal; all the bridges were blown, but they managed to force a crossing and by 1200 hrs next day a Class 9 bridge was across and operating near Vlake. By this time Can 4th Armd Div had captured Bergen-op-Zoom. The clearing of South Beveland continued quickly and on 30 October they reached the eastern end of the causeway over to Walcheren Island. A force was then dispatched to ensure that North Beveland was also clear of enemy.

While Phase 2 was taking place operations on 'Breskens Island' had also continued successfully, so that by nightfall on 1 November, Cadzand and Knokke had been liberated and only the area between the canal

Right: One of the LCTs on its way to Walcheren. These were the same landing craft as had carried men of the 3rd British Inf Div onto Queen Beach on D-Day. (Author's Collection).

and Zeebrugge remained to be cleared, and was accomplished by 3 November. The whole southern bank of the Scheldt estuary was now in Allied hands, after some of the fiercest fighting ever experienced by 21st Army Group. It now remained to clear the island of Walcheren.

Phase 3. Walcheren had a garrison of some 6–7,000 manning the heavy coastal batteries, many of which were housed in massive concrete emplacements and covered the entrance to the West Scheldt. West and south of the island were extensive underwater obstacles, and there were masses of wire and mines on the beaches and beach exits. Flushing had a perimeter defence system with a double line of anti-tank ditches. As in the rest of the area, the terrain was difficult – dikes and steep banks – which ruled out an airborne landing. But if the sea dikes were breached the entire island could be 'sunk', rendering many of the artillery positions untenable and restricting troop movement except in amphibious vehicles – so an assault force thus equipped would be able to take the defences in rear. Early in October, Bomber Command carried out a highly accurate strike, breaching the sea dikes in four places. These gaps were gradually widened by further bombing during the month, so that by the end of October the island had been gradually flooded. The most important gap was near Westkapelle and was some 110 yards wide by about 10 feet high above the low water mark.

It was planned to make two seaborne landings on Walcheren by troops carried and supported by Force 'T' (Royal Navy). One force would move from Breskens to take Flushing; the other, sailing from Ostend, would pass through the breach in the dike at Westkapelle

Right: Approaching Westkapelle, which has just been attacked by rocket-firing Typhoons. The Westkapelle Tower can be seen to the left of the smoke. (Author's Collection)

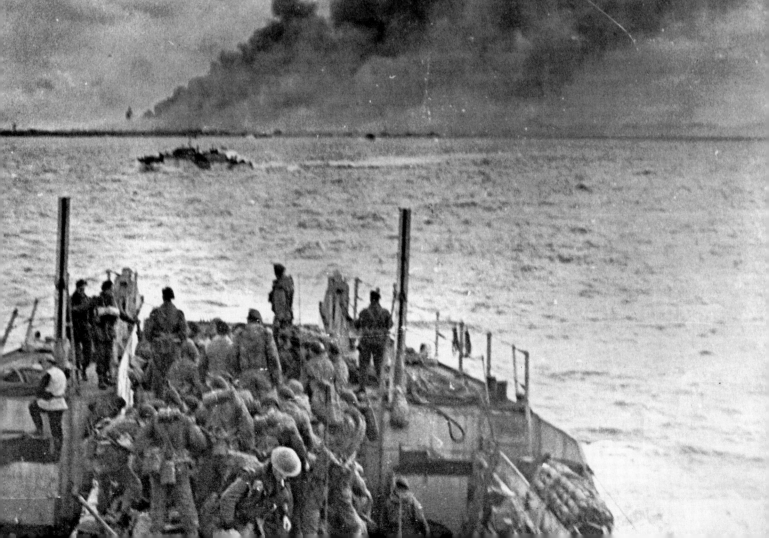

Above: Westkapelle beach. In the foreground is a Weasel – a small amphibious load carrier, whilst behind it is a bogged AVRE, 1 November 1944. (Author's Collection)

Left: German prisoners taken in the fighting on Walcheren Island being housed in a barn on their way to a POW cage. The enemy were mainly from 70 Inf Div, known as the 'Whitebread Division' because many of its soldiers had stomach problems and needed special diets! Nevertheless they fought bravely. (IWM - BU 1267)

to get into the island and link-up with the Flushing attack. In conjunction with the two seaborne landings, a third attack would be made over the South Beveland causeway. The assault began on 1 November. Early in the morning troops of 4 Commando landed near Flushing without suffering many casualties. Luck was on their side because they hit the only section of the shore line near the town which was not mined. They were followed by troops of 52nd Lowland Inf Div in Buffaloes, which came under heavy and accurate fire from 88mm guns and lost some 15 per cent of their strength. The remainder got ashore successfully and the attack pressed on into the town. Ferrying continued throughout the rest of the day, bringing over the leading infantry brigade.

In the meantime, the Westkapelle force was to approach the coast, accompanied by naval forces, with 4 Commando Brigade, less 4

Commando, in the lead. They assaulted the German positions in Westkapelle and on the sand dunes each side of the town, clearing them as far north as Domburg, and southwards until they joined-up with the force attacking Flushing. They were carried in 102 Buffalos manned by 5 ARRE and 11 RTR. Close behind were a mixture of 'Funnies', including two Sherman gun tanks, ten Sherman flails (mineclearing tanks) from 1st Lothians, eight AVREs from 6 ARRE with SBGs (small box girders) and fascines, and four bulldozers, all carried in LCTs which were to beach on the northern side of the breach in the stone-faced dike. The RN Force 'T' included 25 close-support craft (Landing Craft Guns, Landing Craft AA and Landing Craft Rockets). In addition there was a bombardment force consisting of the battleship HMS *Warspite*, and two 15in-gun monitors. Air cover was provided by rocket-firing Typhoons from 85

Right: Dutch commandos who took part in the attack on Flushing march along the waterfront as they take over the port. (IWM - HU 59803)

Group RAF. The force sailed from Ostend at 0100 hrs on 1 November and by 0800 hrs could see Westkapelle Tower shrouded in low rain clouds. The warships opened fire on West-kapelle and Domburg at 0830 hrs, but were hampered by poor visibility and the absence of aircraft spotters. Eventually RA Air OP Austers were used and proved highly successful. The Buffaloes ran ashore protected by the close-support craft of the RN Inshore Squadron which engaged the defences at ranges of less than 1,000 yards, despite heavy and accurate return fire which caused many casualties among the naval craft and the Buffaloes.

The LCTs carrying breaching teams from 79th Armd Div came ashore with the Commandos. Despite heavy fire and many casualties some of the AFVs managed to get ashore and assisted the Commandos in capturing Westkapelle and in operations against the German batteries. The tiny force was not helped by the very high tide which swamped those flails that had landed and left just two Shermans and three AVREs available for further operations. By 8 November, operations had been extended to cover the northern end of the island, where the Domburg battery was knocked out, partly by tank shells fired very accurately through emplacement slits. The assault on Walcheren ended when Middle-burg was captured on the 8th, what was left of the garrison (some 2,000 men) surrendering with their commander, Lieutenant-General Wilhelm Daser. Royal Naval minesweepers began to clear the seaway to Antwerp almost immediately, but it took three weeks of unremitting work by 100 vessels before the 75-mile channel was safe for use, the first convoy berthing at Antwerp on 28 November. The Germans lost many troops in the battle and some 10,000 were taken prisoner. But the Canadians and British had paid a high price – the casualty figure was 27,633, in what Eisen-hower described in his memoirs as being '... a spectacular and gratifying operation'.

Administrative Reorganisation

Now that Antwerp was open, it was possible to shut down the existing Rear Maintenance Area and some of the Channel ports and use their resources in the new Advanced Base. It was planned that Antwerp would receive 40,000 tons of stores a day (exclusive of petrol, oil and lubricants (POL)); 22,500 tons of this total was to be allocated to US forces. There was also plenty of capacity for the handling of bulk fuel, so all would soon be well in that vital area also. But there was still danger to be faced from enemy V-bomb and rocket attacks – the first V-1s and V-2s had landed in Antwerp on 13 October and the port would remain the priority V-bomb target after London, until the launching sites were cleared.

Notes

1. Montgomery, B. *Normandy to the Baltic*
2. Of US origin, the 'Buffalo' was a tracked amphibious craft which could carry 28 men or 4 tons of stores at some 7mph in the water. Its armour could withstand small-arms fire.

Below: Meanwhile, on the mainland, on the road from Tilburg to Breda, Dutch machine gunners keep watch with their British Vickers .303in MG at the ready, to engage any enemy forces withdrawing. (IWM - HU 73791)

8

The 'Lull' before the Storm

Although many of the soldiers who were fighting in most of the armies on the Allied front in North West Europe might not agree, there was definitely something of a lull between the successful opening of the Scheldt estuary to the port of Antwerp, and the start of the Germans' totally unexpected 'last gamble' in the Ardennes. Strictly speaking, this period did not begin until mid-November, and it would last until mid-December, but for the sake of continuity I begin where I ended Chapter 5 (Week 19), because the Scheldt operation only concerned Canadian First Army in particular and 21st Army Group in general; now we must cover activities in the remaining sectors.

Week 20: 17–23 October 1944

In Brussels on the 18th, General Eisenhower held a conference with Montgomery and Bradley to plan future operations. The main conclusions drawn were: that 21st Army Group should continue its operations to open the port of Antwerp as quickly as possible, then launch an attack south-westwards from the Nijmegen bridge-head towards Krefeld. Meanwhile, starting early in November, US First Army would advance to the Rhine near Cologne and gain a bridge-head over the river, with US Ninth Army operating on their left flank. The latter would then attack northwards between the Rhine and the Meuse, so as to link up with British Second Army's

Above: Engineers of 23rd Armd Engr Bn, 3rd Armd Div, US First Army, planting explosive charges in order to blow a gap in this 'Dragons Teeth' anti-tank barrier which was part of the Siegfried Line, 7 October 1944. (US Army via Real War Photos - A 661B)

Below: Tank commander, Cpl Eugene McKay of Illinois, spots an enemy position through his binoculars during the fighting in Aachen. To the left of his Sherman is an M10 tank destroyer. (IWM - EA41436)

Above: Street battle in Aachen. GIs help a wounded comrade to shelter as they follow up tanks mopping up the enemy opposition in house-to-house fighting in the streets of Aachen, 16 October 1944. (IWM - KY 40961)

Right: Infantrymen clamber on board a 3 RTR Sherman, of 11th Armd Div, to advance towards Meerselo and Haag on 17 October 1944. The back decks of a Sherman tank provided a welcome change from foot slogging, but infantry thus carried were more vulnerable to enemy fire than when on the ground. (Tank Museum)

southwards drive. During this part of the operation, US Ninth Army would pass under command of British 21st Army Group. US 12th Army Group was to be responsible for all operations concerning the capture of the Ruhr, while 21st Army Group would determine the feasibility of a northward thrust over the Neder Rijn and on towards the Zuider Zee.

On the 17th, in their drive for Venlo, the leading elements of British Second Army's VII Corps took the Dutch town of Venraij – only 10 miles from the German border, and by the 23rd, XII Corps was attacking towards Tilburg. By the end of the week, 15th Inf Div had reached Tilburg, and 7th Armd and 53rd Inf Divs, followed by 51st Inf Div, were heading for 's Hertogenbosch. Operations were impeded by widespread minefields.

In the adjoining US First Army sector, the German garrison at Aachen was thwarted in its attempts to break out and their resistance

steadily weakened. On the 19th, US 1st Inf and 3rd Armd Divs began a strong assault, taking such vital features as the Lousberg Heights and Salvator Hill, while cutting the Aachen–Laurensburg road. By the 20th, 1st Inf Div had pushed the Germans back into the southern suburbs. At midday on the 21st came the inevitable surrender of what remained of the garrison of the now almost completely ruined city.

In Patton's US Third Army sector bad weather, plus fuel and ammunition shortages, affected operations during this week. US 90th Inf Div was engaged in hand-to-hand fighting in Maizières-lès-Metz. Elsewhere front lines remained unaltered throughout the week.

South of them, in US Seventh Army's sector, XV Corps troops neared Lunéville, some 10 miles south-east of Nancy, while VI Corps – still heavily opposed – reached Bruyères and captured part of the town on the 18th, and the remainder on the 19th. A follow-up division

Above: Bloody Aachen. Crouching behind a knocked-out enemy light anti-aircraft gun mounting in Aachen, Pte William Zukerbrow draws a bead on a Nazi sniper, 19 October 1944. (US Army via Real War Photos - A 465)

(3rd Inf Div) took over the advance towards the next objective – St-Dié – but were soon effectively stopped by strong opposition from German Nineteenth Army. Also in US Seventh Army's sector, two more US divisions (100th and 103rd Inf Divs) landed at Marseilles on the 20th.

In their drive towards the Vosges, troops of French First Army had paused, having sustained heavy casualties.

Week 21: 24–30 October 1944

In Brabant, leading elements of British Second Army had reached 's Hertogenbosch by the 24th, then pushed on beyond, but the Germans launched a counter-offensive. West of Venlo, a sudden, violent attack against US 7th Armd Div (still part of British VIII Corps) forced them out of various positions on the Deurne and Nord Canals.

South of them throughout US 12th Army Group, there was an unexpected lull on all three US Army fronts (First, Ninth, Third). On 22 October, HQ 12th Army Group issued a letter of instruction to all Armies: '12th Army Group will regroup and prepare for an advance by all three Armies to the Rhine River ...' The start date would depend on the weather.

On the 24th, in Third Army, Patton's personal quarters were narrowly missed by three 280mm shells. Also on that date he informed SHAEF that his Army had received more than 2.1 million gallons of fuel *below* their requests and that he now had less than two operational days' fuel left. The 29th saw Maizières-lès-Metz captured, except for the town hall which held out for another day. To make up for his fuel shortages, Patton had instituted aggressive foot patrolling.

Farther south, in US VI Corps' sector of US Seventh Army, 3rd Inf Div had now taken over the push for St-Dié, while units of 45th Inf Div took St-Benoit on the 30th.

Still farther south, on the 24th, General de Lattre de Tassigny prepared his orders for Operation 'Independence', an assault by French First Army on the important Belfort Gap, not far from the Swiss border, which was to be carried out in early November. The attack would take place in conjunction with a general offensive which had three main objectives: to eliminate all German strongpoints west of the Rhine; to establish bridge-heads east of the river; finally, to mount an assault deep into the heart of the Fatherland.

Week 22: 31 October–6 November 1944

On the 31st, British Second Army's XII Corps overcame enemy resistance in the Raamsdonk area. At the end of the week, in British I Corps' sector, Polish 1st Armd Div, supported by units of US 104th Inf Div, began an offensive to take Moerdijk.

In 12th Army Group's area, the long-awaited attack had not yet materialised, having been delayed by bad weather, but all three Army Groups were by now 'rarin' to go!'

In US Third Army's area, US XX Corps troops of 5th Inf Div occupied the Arnaville bridge-head south of Metz, relieving men of 95th Inf Div. US XII Corps crossed the River Seille and captured Abaucourt and Létri-court.

In US Seventh Army's sector, US XV Corps' French 2nd Armd Div entered Bertrichamps on 1 November, US 100th Inf Div arrived in VI Corps' sector to replace 45th Inf Div, while 3rd Inf Div occupied la Bourgonce, north-west of St-Dié, then continued to advance through the Mortagne Forest.

Week 23: 7–13 November 1944

The 'Battle for Germany' officially began at 0600 hrs on 7 November. There was no preparatory aerial bombardment, so tactical surprise was complete. The German High Command had reckoned that the extreme flooding in many areas would prevent any Allied offensive.

In US Third Army's area XII Corps launched their attack with 26th, 35th and 80th Inf Divs advancing simultaneously to the south, centre and north respectively, between Moncourt in the south and Clémery in the north. With excellent counter-battery fire from heavy artillery, they captured Jallaucourt, Malaucourt and Rouves on the first day, as the divisions all raced for the Rhine. At the same time XX Corps launched a massive assault on Metz on the 8th, but this was

Above: US tankers advance into Germany. The crew of an American tank destroyer halt on the road to Vossenach, to check their route. Vossenach is in the Hürtgen Forest, south-east of Aachen, which was recaptured by US First Army troops on 7 November after earlier being forced to evacuate it by a strong German counter-attack. (IWM - EA 46076)

Above: Gen Omar Bradley (left) CG 12th Army Group, visiting US Third Army, 13 November 1944. In the group are Gen George S. Patton, Jr (CG 3rd Army), Maj Gen Paul (CG 26th Inf Div) and Maj Gen Manton Eddy (CG XII Corps on far right). (US Army)

Left: Hürtgen Forest. Men of 3rd Bn, 8th Inf Regt, 3th US Inf Div, move across a small bridge to follow up an M 10 tank destroyer on the track, 18 November 1944. (US Army via Real War Photos - A 232)

hampered by severe flooding in the area of the Moselle. US 5th Inf Div reached Cheminot, south of Metz, 90th Inf Div crossed the river in DUKWs[1] and established a bridge-head near Thionville. On the same day US 6th Armd Div crossed the Seille and prepared for a further advance, as did 10th Armd Div. The weather had improved considerably and US Army Eighth Air Force sent in nearly 1,500 heavy bombers to break the Metz deadlock, hammering away at all the fortified towns east of the bridge-head area: Metz, Verny, Orny, Pommérieux and Saarbrücken, with XIX TAC flying in support. Progress continued on the 10th and 11th, with the enemy fighting delaying actions in the villages and forests. Engineers began building the longest Bailey bridge to date (200ft) at Thionville and two others at Malling, over which poured 10th Armd Div. On 11 November, on Bradley's verbal orders, 83rd Inf Div reverted to US First Army and this move prevented Saarbrücken from being taken – this, in Patton's opinion, was one of the direct causes of the Germans' early success in the Ardennes Offensive.[2]

Week 24: 14–20 November 1944

In 21st Army Group's sector on the 14th, British Second Army's, XII Corps opened an offensive to deal with the German bridge-head over the Maas, between Venlo and Roermond. By the 20th they had made good progress, pushing on towards the river with 49th and 51st Inf Divs.

On the 16th, US Ninth and First Armies launched a co-ordinated offensive (Operation 'Queen') to seize the area north of Aachen, between the Rivers Wurm and Ruhr. Ninth Army's XIX Corps advanced towards the Ruhr with 2nd Armd Div on the left making for Jülich; 29th Inf Div in the centre for Aldenhoven which they captured on the 20th; 30th Inf Div on the right flank for Würselen which they reached on the 17th. A determined counter-attack by German Seventh Army on the 19th was repelled by 2nd Armd Div. Further south, US First Army's VII Corps advanced on Düren (towards Cologne), east of Aachen.

On 18 November US First Army began its advance and bitter campaign in the Hürtgen Forest, penetrating the outer defences of

Düren. This would prove to be one of the most bitterly contested battles of the entire campaign in North West Europe. The Germans had all the advantages of strong defensive terrain; the attacking GIs had to depend almost exclusively on infantry weapons because of the density of the forest and the terrible weather (whenever veterans of the US 4th, 9th and 28th Inf Divs later referred to hard fighting, they did so in terms of comparison with the Battle of the Hürtgen Forest which they put at the top of their list!).

In US Third Army's sector slow and steady progress was made, despite extensive minefields, road-blocks and all manner of other obstacles. On the 14th, leading elements of XII Corps took Haraucourt and Marsal, and further north 6th Armd Div seized Landroff. In XX Corps' area, 95th Inf Div took Ouve-St-Hubert, Fèves and Fort d'Illange, while 10th

Armd Div crossed the Moselle behind a smoke-screen near Thionville and Malling. Further south, on the 15th, 5th Inf Div took Mécleuves in a flanking drive towards Metz, which was now entirely surrounded – six major strong-points were still holding out. On 19 November 5th and 95th Inf Divs finally entered the city and by the 20th it was reported clear of enemy, although certain forts around Metz were still holding out.

In US Seventh Army's sector, XV Corps advanced towards Avricourt and Halloville, while VI Corps broke through enemy positions at Raon-l'Etape, north-west of St-Dié, which other troops were preparing to attack from the south-west. By the end of the week VI Corps' 3rd Inf Div had crossed the Meurthe between Clairefontaine and St-Michel-sur-Meurthe and their large bridge-head included numerous villages.

Below: Geilenkirchen captured. A soldier of US Ninth Army watches Shermans rumbling through the town which was cleared on 19 November, only three days after the US Ninth Army had opened its assault. (IWM - KY 44575)

In the far south, French First Army's I Corps began its offensive towards the Belfort Gap on the 14th, reaching Héricourt, Montbéliard and Hérimoncourt on the 17th. Next day, the leading units were through the Gap and some six miles beyond between the Rhine Canal and Delle on the Swiss border. They reached the outskirts of Belfort on the 19th and by last light were at Rosenau, near Basel, on the Rhine. Fighting continued in Belfort, but meanwhile on the 20th, units of 1st French Armd Div reached Mulhouse.

Week 25: 21–27 November 1944

British Second Army's 49th and 51st Inf Divs were continuing their advance on Venlo, while on 22 November, VIII Corps' 15th Inf Div took the villages of Sevenum and Horst to the north-west of the town. On 26 November V-1's and V-2's hit Antwerp for the first time.

In US Ninth Army's sector, XIX Corps began the final phase of Operation 'Queen'.

In US First Army's sector, VII Corps' 104th Inf Div took Frenz on the 26th, while units of 4th Inf Div consolidated their gains in the Hürtgen Forest area. Mopping-up continued throughout the rest of the week, while 29th Inf Div were similarly occupied on their way to the River Ruhr.

The Germans were still causing US Third Army considerable delay on XII Corps' front, but at Metz, 'The Bastion of the East', the two-month siege ended on 22 November when XX Corps reported it subdued. This opened another route to the German frontier and the Siegfried Line. Despite bad weather, which was hampering air and ground movement, US XII and XX Corps made steady progress east and north-east, 4th Armd Div crossing the Saar on 24 November and 10th Armd Div crossing the

Below: The Battle for Metz. Men of the 95th Inf Div, US Third Army, smash down the door of a house in Metz, during street fighting, 22 November 1944. (US Army via Real War Photos - A 755)

Left: Infantrymen of XII Corps, US Third Army, pass a sign to Saarbrucken as they advance through St Avold, which was liberated on 27 November 1944. (IWM - EA 45644)

Right: The Shermans of US First Army have certainly battered Hürtgen to pieces. It was at an important road junction on the road to Cologne, in the middle of the Hürtgen Forest and was captured 28 November 1944. (IWM EA 46073)

Right: Engineers of 24th Engineers, 4th Armd Div, US Third Army, carrying out the unenviable task of clearing a dirt road of mines. One man has already been killed. 1 December 1944. (US Army via Real War Photos - A 504)

German border on the 25th to capture Bethingen.

In US Seventh Army's sector, 2nd Armd Div was advancing towards Saverne from Bouxwiller and Birkenwald, while 100th Inf Div took Senones on the 22nd and pushed on towards St-Blaise; on the same day 3rd Inf Div took St-Dié. On the 27th 100th Inf Div arrived in the Saarebourg area, and General Eisenhower ordered General Patch's Army to swing north to assist General Patton's troops to capture the Saar basin. On that day too, VI Corps' 3rd Inf Div replaced French 2nd Armd Div in Strasbourg.

On the 22nd 1st Inf Div of French First Army's II Corps, took Giromagny, opening up a gap along the River Savoreuse, and I Corps entered Mulhouse, close to the German border. On the 24th, troops of both US I and II Corps were ordered to converge on Burnhaupt as quickly as possible so as to force an enemy withdrawal into Alsace.

Week 26: 28 November–4 December 1944

By 30 November, in south-east Holland, British Second Army's VIII and XIX Corps had cleared the enemy's bridge-head over the Maas, only a small pocket remaining near Blerick. On 2 December the Germans blew a dike on the lower Rhine near Arnhem, causing severe flooding and forcing Can First Army's II Corps to withdraw over the Waal. British Second Army's XII Corps captured Blerick (opposite Venlo on the Maas) on 3 December, thus clearing the entire region west of the river.

In US Ninth Army's sector, XIII Corps continued to advance towards Linnich which

102nd Inf Div took on 1st December; they reached the River Ruhr two days later. On the 4th they broke off their offensive, having taken all their objectives west of the River Ruhr except the villages of Würm and Müllendorf.

US First Army's VII and V Corps continued their difficult operations in the Hürtgen Forest and in the River Inde sector, VII Corps reaching the vicinity of Lammersdorf and Inden on the 30th. On 3 December troops of 5th Armd Div reached Brandenberg and reinforced their bridge-head over the river next day.

US Third Army's XII and XX Corps made steady progress in their attacks against the 'West Wall', despite continuing bad weather which restricted armoured vehicles to the roads. The enemy made full use of obstacles, including, for example, old Maginot Line positions. On the 29th XII Corps regrouped, and its 4th and 6th Armd Divs probed into the Saar and took high ground in the corps area, while XX Corps troops continued to make progress within Germany. US III Corps remained non-operational at Etain. On 30 November, 6th Cavalry Group was formed – soon to be known as 'Patton's Household Cavalry'! At the end of the week III Corps' 87th Inf Div took over from 5th Inf Div in the Metz area, with the task of containing those forts that were still holding out, including Fort Jeanne d'Arc. Sarre-Union was cleared on the 4th.

Farther south in US Seventh Army's area, French 2nd Armd Div (VI Corps) reached Erstein, about 10 miles SW of Strasbourg, on the 28th, but was halted by determined resistance. US XV Corps' 79th Inf Div captured Schweigenhause in Alsace on 1 December, while 44th and 45th Inf Divs were engaged in heavy fighting near Tiffenbach and Zinswiller, managing to take the latter on the 3rd.

In the far south, French First Army, reinforced by the arrival of US 76th Inf Div on 2 December, began an operation to squeeze out the Colmar pocket by converging attacks from north and south.

Above: Maj Gen Maurice Rose, dynamic CG of 3rd Armd Div from August 1944 until 31 March 1945, when he was killed in action, is seen here beside his Jeep at Zweifall, 30 November 1944. (US Army via Patton Museum)

Right: A massive 240 mm MI howitzer belonging to US Ninth Army is seen in action during the drive on Germany, 12 December 1944. The 360lb shell could be delivered out to 23,000 metres. (US Army via Real War Photos - A 3167)

Below: A platoon of three HMC M8s of US First Army, in action in the Hürtgen Forest area on 7 December 1944. The HMC M8 mounted a 75mm howitzer on the chassis of an M5 light tank, to make a very effective small HMC; nearly 1,780 were built and used in HQ Companies of medium tank battalions until replaced by 105mm howitzers. (US Army via Real War Photos - A 209)

Week 27: 5–11 December 1944

On 10 December US First Army's VII Corps launched an attack between the Rivers Inde and Ruhr to take Düren, using 9th, 83rd and 104th Inf Divs, plus 3rd Armd Div.

In US Third Army's sector, XII Corps' 4th Armd Div seized an intact bridge over the River Eichel at Vollerdingen and established a small bridge-head. In XX Corps's area 95th Inf Div encountered heavy street fighting in Saarlauten, but managed to establish a bridge-head at Lisdorf. On the 8th, 35th Inf Div crossed the Saar in four places. Bad weather restricted flying, but, significantly, air recce reports indicated a build-up of enemy forces in the Eifel area. On the 9th G-2 sent a report to SHAEF that a major enemy assault in the Ardennes was probable, but this was ignored.[3]

US Seventh Army deployed two corps in an advance towards the Maginot and Siegfried Lines.

In the far south, on 6 December French First Army's I Corps began an attack on the Colmar pocket, while II Corps was facing heavy counter-attacks in the area of Ostheim, Guemar and Mittelwihr; the latter was taken on the 9th after heavy fighting. By 10 December, I Corps' 2nd Moroccan Div had taken Thann and 9th Colonial Div had eliminated all enemy west of the Rhine between Kembs and the Swiss border.

Week 28: 12–18 December 1944

(See Chapter 9 for an account of the Battle of the Bulge – 16 December 1944–20 January 1945)

Above: A mortar crew in action near the Hürtgen Forest, 13 December 1944. (US Army via Real War Photos - A 203)

Left: Men of a heavy weapons platoon set up their .30 cal M1917A1 Browning machine gun in Saarlauten, during heavy fighting there. The M1917A1 was the drastically revised model of the original M1917 machine gun, and was the standard support MG of the US Army throughout WWII. (IWM - EA 53153)

THE 'LULL' BEFORE THE STORM

US First Army began the week by taking Pier and forcing the enemy to withdraw over the Ruhr. Having taken most of the area between the Inde and the Ruhr, VII Corps operations were concluded, while 104th Inf Div reached the Ruhr on a 4½-mile front. Both US First and Third Armies' operations ceased on the 14th and there was a lull.

On 12 December US Third Army's G-2 sent yet another warning to SHAEF about a dangerous enemy build-up opposite US First Army and the likelihood of a major German offensive in the Ardennes. Patton quietly began his own planning so that he would be ready if and when the balloon went up – which of course it did on the 16th.

US Seventh Army was halted at Hottviller–Bitche on the Maginot Line, while to its south, French First Army was attacking positions west of the Rhine in the Colmar pocket.

Operations virtually came to a halt along the entire front as attention focused on the possibility of a German assault in the Ardennes.

Notes

1. DUKW = Truck, Amphibious 2½-ton 6x6, which used its normal drive on land and had a rudder and propeller for use in water.

2. Patton was to record that he considered this to be one of the major errors of the entire campaign. 'If Bradley had not welshed on his agreement,' he wrote in his diary, 'we would have taken Saarbrücken within 48 hrs after we got Koenigsmacker. Once we had [Koenigsmacker] they couldn't have stopped us from taking Trier, and if we'd had Trier it would have been impossible for the Germans to launch their Ardennes offensive.'

3. US Third Army's G-2 Section reported on a significant enemy build-up, and its after-action report for the period 3–10 December 1944 included the statement (written at the time): 'Overall the initiative rests with the Allies, but the massive Armored force the enemy has built up in reserve gives him the definite capability of launching a spoiling (diversionary) offensive to disrupt the Allies' drive.' It was ignored by SHAEF.

Below: This heavy machine gun crew are carrying their .50 cal Browning machine gun into a shell-pocked building in Saarlauten. Like the .30 cal Browning, the .50 is still in service worldwide. (IWM - EA 53096)

Left: Winter mud. A 'Jimmy' (GMC 2ton) struggles through thick winter mud, somewhere in Belgium, before the winter snow came in late 1944. (Tank Museum)

Left: Metz. German prisoners march out of Fort Jeanne d'Arc at Metz, following its capitulation to US Third Army on 13 December 1944. (IWM - EA 47508)

Left: Metz. Maj Gen Walton Walker, CG XX Corps, leaving the town hall in Metz after formally handing back the liberated city to its citizens. (IWM - EA 45037)

9

Hitler's Ardennes Offensive

(Week 28 (12–18 December 1944) to Week 33 (16–22 January 1945)

Wacht am Rhein

'Soldiers of the West Front! Your great hour has arrived. Large attacking armies have started to advance against the Anglo–Americans. I do not have to tell you anything more than that. You feel it yourselves. *We are gambling everything!* You carry with you the holy obligation to give everything to achieve things beyond human possibilities for our Fatherland and our Führer!' Field Marshal Gerd von Rundstedt's message to his troops.

It was as early as mid-September that Adolf Hitler had first astounded his generals when, after a normal 'Führer conference', he had

Right: Overall Commander of the German forces for the assault was Field Marshal Gerd von Rundstedt, who had been reinstated as OB West in September 1944. When he first heard of Hitler's proposals, he was staggered by the scale of the operation, had grave misgivings, but was forced to go along with it. (IWM - AP 47832)

invited Field Marshal Keitel and Generals Jodl, Guderian and Kreipe (representing Göring) into an inner chamber where, as they discussed the current position of the war, the name 'Ardennes' had been mentioned and Hitler had come to life. 'Raising his hand, he had exclaimed: "Stop!" There was a dead pause. Finally Hitler spoke: "I have made a momentous decision. I am taking the offensive. Here – out of the Ardennes!" He smashed his fist on the unrolled map before him. "Across the Meuse and on to Antwerp!" The others stared in wonder. His shoulders squared, his eyes luminous, the signs of care and sickness gone. This was the dynamic Hitler of 1940.'[1]

The plan for this daring operation was undoubtedly Hitler's brainchild. It was code-named *'Wacht am Rhein'* (Watch on the Rhine), so as to mislead Allied intelligence, and when he sent copies to von Rundstedt (reinstated as OB West in September) and Model (Commander Army Group B) he is supposed to have personally marked the cover: 'NOT TO BE ALTERED'! In essence, the plan consisted of an early morning (0530 hrs) assault by three armies, striking through the Ardennes between Monschau in the north and Echternach in the south – a frontage of some 85 miles. After crossing the River Meuse between Liège and Namur, the assault would bypass Brussels and aim at capturing Antwerp within a week. The American and British forces, now cut in two, would never be able to recover from the shock and would have to make a separate peace, leaving Germany free to deal with the Soviet Union. The German High Command (OKW) were secretly appalled by the plan, but, in the aftermath of the unsuccessful attempt on the Führer's life, no one dared to argue. Hitler chose tough SS General 'Sepp' Dietrich to play a leading role.

His Sixth SS Panzer Army would be in the north of the assault force, to its left was to be General Baron Hasso von Manteuffel's Fifth Panzer Army, with General der Panzertruppen Erich Bradenberger's weaker Seventh Army, protecting the southern flank of the operation. Field Marshal Model would be in overall operational control. When von Rundstedt heard about the scale of the operation he was staggered by its size and scope, and, considering it far too ambitious, proposed a more limited attack to take out the Allied salient around Aachen, but this was dismissed by Hitler and the OKW. Post-war he commented: 'It was then only up to me to obey. It was a nonsensical operation and the most stupid part was setting Antwerp as the target. If we reached the Meuse we should have got down on our knees and thanked God – let alone tried to have reached Antwerp.'[2] There was also opposition to the plan from Dietrich, who took his complaints to Jodl, Chief of Staff OKW, but got nowhere. His SS panzer divisions were to make the main effort, while the Army

panzer divisions would only play a supporting role – a deliberate slap in the eye for the Army, whose officers had tried to kill Hitler.

Von Manteuffel was a tough, loyal commander, but like von Rundstedt and Dietrich he did not hold out much hope of getting beyond the Meuse. He would show his personal bravery early on in the operation, going out disguised as an intelligence colonel and personally directing the intensive patrolling that took place before the attack. Erich Bradenberger, despite his 'unheroic appearance' – he looked more like a schoolmaster – had already proved himself a competent commander when he took over as Seventh Army commander from Gen Heinrich Eberbach when the latter was captured (28 August 1944), but he was nevertheless worried about his role on the southern flank, being short of tanks and facing Patton's Third Army for whom the Germans had developed a healthy respect. In round figures the Germans had assembled some 250,000 men, nearly 2,000 guns and 1,000 tanks, making it the

Above left: Playing a major role in the assault was the rough, tough SS General Josef 'Sepp' Dietrich. Hitler deliberately gave his Sixth Panzer Army the major role in the assault, as a snub to the Army for failing to protect him properly in the unsuccessful bomb plot to kill him. (Tank Museum)

Above: Field Marshal Walter Model commanded Heersgruppe B during the Ardennes Offensive, and, with von Rundstedt, was sent a copy of Hitler's 'Wacht am Rhein' supposedly marked personally by Hitler: 'Not to be altered'! (IWM MH 12850)

Above: CG of 12th Army Group was Gen Omar Bradley (here photographed in London just after VE-Day). Gen Hodges' First Army was part of his Army Group as was Gen Patton's Third Army to the south and Gen Simpson's Ninth to the north. (Author's Collection)

shortly to receive its first taste of battle; south of them was 28th Inf Div which was recovering from the fighting in the Hürtgen Forest where it had sustained heavy casualties. The other two divisions in VIII Corps were the 'green' 9th Armd Div, which was to support the Roer dams operation and for whom the coming battle would be their first major operation, and 4th Inf Div, also recovering in Luxembourg after the Hürtgen Forest campaign.

The Plan

In the north, the first wave of Dietrich's SS Sixth Panzer Army, comprising four infantry (12th, 277th, 326th Volksgrenadier Divs (VGD) and 3rd Parachute Div) and two SS Pz Divs (1st (*Leibstandarte Adolf Hitler*) and 12th (*Hitler Jugend*) were concentrated on a narrow front between Monschau and the Losheim Gap. In this group was also Otto Skorzeny's *ad hoc* Commando brigade (150th Pz Bde). The infantry was to lead initially, striking into the sparse road network of the Ardennes, advancing some 3–5 miles on the first morning and thus opening the way for the tanks to pass through and head with all speed for the Meuse. The armour would be led by 1st SS Pz Div whose 140+ AFVs (including many Panthers and Tigers) made it the most powerful German unit in the Ardennes. It was confidently assumed that the leading tanks would reach the Meuse and seize a crossing by the end of the fourth day. South of this major assault, von Manteuffel's Fifth Pz Army had two primary objectives: to encircle the forward elements of US 106th Inf Div in the Schnee-Eifel and advance to capture the key town of St. Vith. This would be the main task for two of the infantry divisions. Secondly, two infantry and three panzer divisions would secure crossings over the River Our further south, then go like hell, parallel with Dietrich's leading elements, all the way to Antwerp! As the first problem concerned bridging the Our, the infantry would lead, establish its bridgeheads and protect the engineers while they erected suitable tank bridges across the river. Finally, to the south of the two panzer Armies, Seventh Army, the weakest of the three armies,

most formidable fighting force ever to face the British and Americans in one single operation. They were to be supported by some 1,500 aircraft of the Luftwaffe's *Jagdkorps II* – about half the number Göring had originally promised.

Facing them in the Ardennes sector were just six divisions of V and VIII Corps in General Courtney Hodges' US First Army. On the left flank was V Corps' 2nd Inf Div, veterans who were preparing for an assault on the dams of the Rivers Roer and Urft. They had been holding the St. Vith area, but were relieved on 11 December by VIII Corps' 106th Inf Div, so that they could take part in the attack on the dams. The other division in V Corps was 99th Inf Div a recently arrived formation (entered the line 9 November), which began the assault on the dams on 13 December against heavy opposition. They would both be hit hard by the totally unexpected German assault. South of them was General Troy Middleton's VIII Corps with the 'green' 106th Inf Div now in the line and

would capture a bridge-head, again over the Our, between Vianden and Echternach, then advance westwards, keeping station, so as to protect von Manteuffel's left flank against possible attacks from US Third Army.

The Germans were hoping that the weather would remain bad enough to ground Allied aircraft, although they had assembled more Luftwaffe support than for any previous operation on the Allied front.

Deception

Following the Allied example after the success of the Operation 'Fortitude' deception plan, the Germans took many precautions to conceal the nature of 'Wacht am Rhein' – even the code-name was deliberately chosen so as to sound defensive. Troops, weapons and equipment were only moved by night. Troop positions were carefully camouflaged, and only smoke-less charcoal fires were permitted in the

Left: CG of the US First Army was Lt Gen Courtney Hodges – seen here with Gen Eisenhower. Also in the front row are Patton and Bradley on Ike's right and Simpson on the far left of Hodges. The photograph was taken in Belgium on 10 October 1944. (IWM - AP 44557)

Right: Attack! Although this was definitely a posed photograph, it does have dramatic impact, as an SS Rottenführer orders his men to attack. The photograph was one of a sequence taken after an actual battle between men of Kampfgruppe Hansen of I SS Pz Div and 14th Cav Group, US 7th Armd Div, north of Poteau. Destroyed American vehicles form the backdrop. (IWM - EA 47959)

Left: Bastogne before the siege began. The photograph shows vehicles and men of Combat Command B (normally just called 'CCB') of 10th Armd Div arriving in the main street of Bastogne on 18 December 1944. It was then split into three combat groups and sent to help close the main routes towards the town from the north-east. (IWM - EA 48295)

forward areas which were strictly policed by special security detachments. Even the leading troops were kept unaware of what was actually planned until the night before the attack. The Germans had great faith in their ENIGMA cipher machine, unaware that it had been broken by the Allies years ago. Believing that the Allies were obtaining information from spies and traitors, extra precautions were taken and most of the planning orders were delivered by hand so that for this operation ENIGMA had few secrets to yield. The Germans also intended to use groups of specially trained English-speaking Commandos dressed and equipped in American uniforms and driving captured American vehicles, to infiltrate

137

behind Allied lines, blow up dumps, attack headquarters, kill troops and civilians, cut telephone lines, and generally spread panic. This was the primary task of Otto Skorzeny's 150th Panzer Brigade. It was also intended to drop paratroops in depth, so as to block the movement of American reinforcements southwards.

The Assault

As planned, a barrage of shells and rockets landed on the American positions just before first light on 16 December, heralding the opening of the largest and most important battle of the Allied campaign in Europe. In the north, the two VGDs of I SS Pz Corps mounted a heavy attack against the green troops of 99th Inf Div, but instead of caving in, the GIs fought with great bravery and, despite heavy

casualties, held their positions all day and throughout the night. To their south, von Manteuffel's chosen location for crossing the Our was directly opposite the veteran 28th Inf Div, which had suffered heavy casualties in the Hürtgen Forest. In places the Germans had a numerical advantage of more than 10 to 1, and dense fog and the deliberate absence of a long, preparatory barrage (although when it came it was extremely heavy), allowed the assault force to get within yards of the US positions, in some places before they were detected. Nevertheless, just as in the 99th Inf Div sector, the Americans fought bravely, the key villages of Marnach and Hosingen holding out all day. But many German troops were bypassing the US positions and disappearing westwards, moving deeper into the forests.

Furthermore, the pioneers had managed to complete tank bridges at Dasburg and Gemund, so that the panzers could get across the Our and debouch westwards. US VIII Corps' commander, General Middleton, had been planning to conduct a fighting withdrawal in the event of an enemy offensive, but changed his plan once the battle had begun and instead, ordered his beleaguered troops to defend their positions for as long as possible.

A Breakthrough

Against this determined defence, the German assault was soon falling seriously behind schedule, everywhere that is except in the area of the Losheim Gap, on almost exactly the same route which the Germans had used when they invaded France and Belgium in 1940. The approximately seven-mile gap was the most lightly held section of the entire front line. It also was close to the inter-corps boundary between US V Corps in the north and VIII Corps in the south. Nevertheless, the outnumbered Americans did their best to hold the panzers back and did so until first light the following day (17th), when Tiger tanks made a breakthrough. To the immediate south of the Losheim Gap, the GIs in the Schnee-Eifel area were also now under heavy attack and very vulnerable, and a two-pronged attack also threatened the key road centre of St. Vith. Thus, by the morning of the 17th, it was clear that the Germans had torn two gaps through the US line – one on 106th Inf Div's front (Schnee-Eifel), the other on 28th Inf Div's front. Reports were confusing, but it was apparent that enemy armour was now progressing rapidly westwards. In addition, German Seventh Army had made some progress, crossing the Sauer and establishing a

Below: GIs struggle to reposition their M1 57mm anti-tank gun in a forward area on the Germany/Belgium border in order to try to help stem the German onslaught. (IWM - EA 48040)

number of bridge-heads. Hitler was reportedly delighted with the results to date, the weather was still 'Hitler weather' – fog, drizzle and haze, and it was forecast to continue, while his ground forces appeared to be advancing as per plan: 'Everything has changed in the West!' he exclaimed. 'Success – complete success – is now in our grasp!'

Allied Reaction

When General Hodges first heard of the German attacks (at about 0700 hrs on the 16th), he had put a reserve Regimental Combat Team on full alert and a few hours later ordered 9th Armd Div to release their CCA from the Roer dams attack and send it to support VIII Corps. Apart from this he did little, not realising that this was a major enemy assault and not just a spoiling attack to counter the Roer dams assault. Middleton, however, was in no doubt that this was a major offensive and requested reinforcements. There was considerable delay in releasing anything: for a number of reasons: the Allied High Command did not want to put off the Roer dams assault or postpone future planned operations; there were only four uncommitted US divisions, two of which were airborne; they were not convinced that this was a major assault. Eisenhower, however, sensed that something big was taking place: 'I was immediately convinced that this was no local attack,' he wrote in his memoirs. 'It was not logical for the enemy to attempt merely a minor offensive in the Ardennes ... We had always been convinced that before the Germans acknowledged final defeat in the west they would attempt one desperate counter-offensive.'[3] He recommended that Bradley send in two armoured divisions – 7th from the north and 10th from the south and earmark US 82nd and 101st Ab Divs (resting and rehabilitating after the Arnhem operations) as immediate reinforcements. They would be on their way to the Ardennes next day: 82nd to the Houffalize sector at the very centre of von Manteuffel's assault, 101st to Bastogne, the most important road junction in the region. On Sixth SS Pz Army's front the German

attack was being contained in the area of the Monschau–Elsenborn Ridge by those elements of 2nd and 99th Inf Divs that had pulled back and joined with the veteran 1st Inf Div to form a tough defensive position, fortunately with plenty of artillery on call. On Hitler's direct orders the Germans would continue to attack here without success until Christmas Eve. Farther south, in the Losheim Gap, the Germans had more success, reaching Trois-Points on the River Amblève by the 19th, then advancing northwards towards Spa. But they were held, and a counter-attack by 82nd Ab Div pushed them back over the river where they dug in. One of the leading elements of 1st SS Pz Div was Obersturmbannführer Joachim Peiper's battlegroup which comprised some 100 tanks (Panthers and Mk IVs) plus a fully motorised panzergrenadier unit. Peiper would gain infamous notoriety, by shooting 85 American prisoners just south of Malmédy – an act which he thought was in

Below: The skies clear, 23 December 1944. Gen Patton's prayer for fine weather was certainly answered and the skies cleared on the 23rd for some six days, giving US Third Army plenty of clear weather for battle. Patton presented his padre with a Bronze Star, telling him: '... You sure stand in good with the Lord and the soldiers!' Here GIs watch an aerial dogfight over the snowcovered Ardennes. (IWM - EA 49742)

keeping with his role of spreading alarm and despondency among the Americans. In fact it had the directly opposite effect of stiffening the GIs' resolve everywhere. By 25 December, the attack by Dietrich's much vaunted SS Army had virtually ground to a halt and they had gone on to the defensive.

In the central sector, von Manteuffel's Fifth Panzer Army was still advancing, a major objective being St. Vith. Here, Colonel Bruce Clarke, then commanding CCB of 7th Armd Div, took over command of a hodgepodge of units in the area and rapidly welded them into a cohesive fighting force, capable of holding off all enemy thrusts until 23 December, using mobile 'hit and retire tactics', delaying the enemy's advance so that their carefully timed

programme was soon in tatters. After the war von Manteuffel said that he had thought he was being opposed by a far larger force, while 'Clarke of St. Vith', as he came to be called, said: 'As the commander of CCB, I analysed the situation and decided that the probable objective of the German attack was not just St. Vith or a bridge-head over the Salm River, but rather a decisive objective far to my rear, probably toward the English Channel. I could well afford to be forced back slowly, surrendering a few kilometres of terrain at a time to the German forces while preventing the destruction of my command and giving other units to my rear the time to prepare a defence and a counter-attack. Therefore by retiring a kilometre a day, I was winning, and the Germans,

Above: The relief of Bastogne. Jeeps and half-tracks belonging to 25th Cav Regt, US 4th Armd Div, pass dead GIs on the road near Chaumont, Luxembourg, where they were killed in the desperate race to reach Bastogne and relieve the garrison there. 27 December 1944. (US Army via Real War Photos - A 501)

Above: Men of 137th Regt, 35 Inf Div, advancing towards the Luxembourg border from Tintange in Belgium, in their drive to cut off the German advance. 27 December 1944 (US Army via Real War Photos - A 3179)

by being prevented from advancing many kilometres or so a day, were losing.'[4]

While Clarke was performing miracles at St. Vith, farther south other panzer spearheads were closing up on the equally vital road hub of Bastogne. It too would become a focal point of the American defence in the Ardennes. But when Eisenhower held an emergency meeting on the evening of the 19th, it looked as though the enemy were going hell for leather between Bastogne and St. Vith, across the Ourthe and on towards the Meuse. At the meeting Patton alone was all for letting the enemy outreach himself and then 'chewing him up'.[5] Bradley and Eisenhower were adamant that the enemy must not be allowed to cross the Meuse; indeed, it was at this junc-

ture that Eisenhower instructed Montgomery to take command of US First and Ninth Armies north of the salient, and to halt the enemy and oppose him with a firm front in conjunction with 12th Army Group to the south. Monty immediately deployed XXX Corps in a blocking position on the Meuse, while deploying Hodges to contain the northern shoulder of the enemy thrust.

Not content with calling a halt to the German thrusts, Eisenhower wanted at the same time to launch a major counter-attack, ideally from the south. He asked Patton when he could attack and with what force. He didn't know that GSP had been looking at the situation for some days and preparing for just such an emergency, so his confident reply: 'On

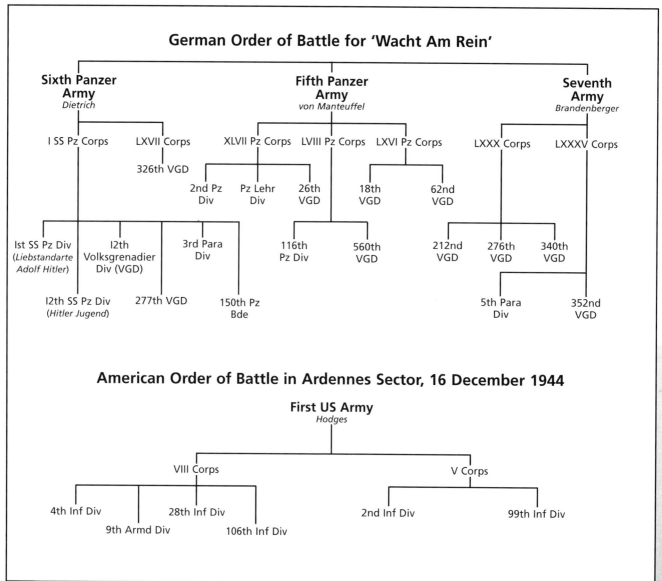

German Order of Battle for 'Wacht Am Rein'

Sixth Panzer Army
Dietrich

Fifth Panzer Army
von Manteuffel

Seventh Army
Brandenberger

I SS Pz Corps — LXVII Corps

XLVII Pz Corps — LVIII Pz Corps — LXVI Pz Corps

LXXX Corps — LXXXV Corps

326th VGD

2nd Pz Div — Pz Lehr Div — 26th VGD

18th VGD — 62nd VGD

Ist SS Pz Div (*Liebstandarte Adolf Hitler*) — 12th Volksgrenadier Div (VGD) — 3rd Para Div

116th Pz Div — 560th VGD

212nd VGD — 276th VGD — 340th VGD

12th SS Pz Div (*Hitler Jugend*) — 277th VGD — 150th Pz Bde

5th Para Div — 352nd VGD

American Order of Battle in Ardennes Sector, 16 December 1944

First US Army
Hodges

VIII Corps

V Corps

4th Inf Div — 9th Armd Div — 28th Inf Div — 106th Inf Div

2nd Inf Div — 99th Inf Div

December 22, with three divisions, the 4th Armored, the 26th and the 80th,' came as a complete shock and was as Martin Blumenson says in the 'Patton Papers': 'the sublime moment of his [GSP's] career'. The assault was also aimed at relieving Bastogne, where 101st Airborne was now under siege. Their epic defence lasted until the equally epic advance of CCR, 4th Armd Div, broke through on 26 December.

Meanwhile, the main body of the German armies were pushing on towards the Meuse. In the north 116th Pz Div crossed the Ourthe at Hotton, but were then halted by US 84th Inf Div. To their south the crack *Panzer Lehr* Division reached as far as Ciergnon, some twelve miles from Dinant and the Meuse, while 2nd Pz Div occupied Foy-Notre-Dame, only a tantalising four miles from the river on 24 December. This was the limit of the German advance after which '*Wacht am Rhein*' collapsed. The leading panzers were now some 60 miles from their start lines, short of everything, crews exhausted, and surrounded by their enemies who were not only starting to mount counter-attacks but were also unleashing the full weight of their devastating air attacks from the rapidly clearing skies. There was nothing to do but retreat and they were harried all the way. Requests to be allowed to make an orderly withdrawal were denied by Hitler; in fact, as von Manteuffel wrote later:

'Instead of ordering a timely withdrawal, we were forced to retire yard by yard, under the pressure of the attacking Allies, suffering useless losses.' On 16 January, US Third Army linked up with Hodges' US First Army northeast of Bastogne, and the battle was over.

'The battle of the Ardennes was won primarily by the staunch fighting qualities of the American soldier.' That testimonial came from one of their severest critics – Montgomery. And it was not idle praise. Nevertheless victory had been won at great expense on both sides – the Americans lost more than 10,000 men killed, nearly 48,000 wounded and 23,000 missing. German losses were even higher – some sources put the figure as high as 120,000. There was also a high loss of AFVs on both sides, but whereas the Allies could quickly replace their losses, the 600 plus panzers which had been destroyed could not be so easily replaced. The Ardennes offensive had delayed the Allied advance into Germany by some three weeks, but had undoubtedly brought the end of the war much nearer.

Notes

1. Toland, J. *Adolf Hitler*.
2. Brett-Smith, R. *Hitler's Generals*.
3. Eisenhower, D. *Crusade in Europe*.
4. Clarke, General Bruce. 'The Battle for St Vith', in *Armor Magazine*, November-December 1974
5. At the meeting Patton said: 'Hell let's have the guts to let the sons of bitches go all the way to Paris. Then we'll really cut 'em up and chew 'em up!' Needless to say Ike went for a more cautious approach which did not allow the enemy to cross the Meuse.

Below: Armoured Infantry of 53rd Armd Inf Bn, US Third Army, move forward to attack the Germans who are surrounding Bastogne. Together with 37th Tank Bn, also of 4th Armd Div, the 53rd spearheaded the relief of Bastogne. (IWM EA 48751)

Top left: New Year's Day and vehicles belonging to 11 Armd Div prepare for an attack on the outskirts of Bastogne. Closest to the camera is an M3 half-track. (IWM - EA 48742)

Left: Covering the Bastogne corridor. A Browning machine gun crew of 10th Infantry, 4th Armd Div look out of their foxhole, over the snow-covered fields of the Ardennes near Bastogne, covering an advancing Sherman in the Bastogne corridor. 3 January 1945. (US Army)

Above: Bazookamen of 3rd Armd Div, US First Army, in a snow-covered foxhole near the Ardennes forest, await enemy armour, 14 January 1945, probably in vain. With a maximum range of 700yds, the M1 Bazooka could penetrate 4.7in of armour. Nearly half a million were produced during the war. (US Army via Real War Photos - A 660B)

Right: Noville, near Bastogne, 16 January 1945. Gen Maxwell Taylor, commander of 101st Ab Div, confers with senior officers of the division. (IWM - EA 50507)

10
To the Rhine

Into the Rhineland

The campaign which began as soon as the German Ardennes offensive had been effectively dealt with was to prove a very varied one which, as the US official history says, had: '... gathered its momentum in the snows of the Ardennes and the mud and pillboxes of the West Wall'. The fighting would be every bit as hard as any that had gone before, as the Germans tried desperately – but with little real chance of success – to defend their Führer and their Fatherland, while the American, British, Canadian and French armies continued to push them back from the Siegfried Line defences, taking every advantage of the heavy losses the enemy had suffered. The Allies would have

to face several more months of fighting, which would include not only the capture of thousands of prisoners, the taking of acres and acres of enemy territory and the occupation of hundreds of ruined towns and cities, but such major events as the crossing of the Rhine; the release of Allied POWs and the full realisation of the horrors of the Nazi concentration camps; the successful link-ups with the Red Army on the Elbe; and the final shambles in Berlin with the death of Adolf Hitler and the end of the Third Reich. On the other side of Germany, the Red Army was continuing its victorious winter drive to the Oder – launched in mid-January 1945 – which would lead to eventual victory in the east as well.

Below: Men of XII Corps advance further into Germany. At dawn on 15 January 1945, 4/5 Royal Scots Fusiliers, 156 Bde of 52 Inf Div, put in an attack towards Stein from Tuddern. Here men of 11 Pl, B Coy, are firing at the withdrawing enemy from trenches in Stein. (IWM - B 13793)

Above: XII Corps attack continues. Infantrymen of 6th Cameronians advancing from Tuddern, north of Sittard. Note the group of AFVs to their right; the nearest is a Sherman Crab, mine flail, used to gap minefields. 18 January 1945. (IWM B 13782)

Below: XII Corps attack. Near Echt, troops of 5 KOSB, 131 Bde of 7th Armd Div, move past a group of German POWs – they are Luftwaffe personnel, behind whom are some British armoured cars. (IWM - B 13751)

Left: XII Corps attack. Troops of the 6th Cameronians, advancing towards the village of Havert from Tuddern, pass a column of Sherman tanks, Bren gun carriers and other AFVs in Tuddern. All the AFVs have been whitewashed to blend with the snow. The second Sherman is a Firefly, as can be seen by the shape of its muzzle break just sticking above the rear of the leading tank. 18 January 1945. (IWM - B 13767)

Right: Men of 9 DLI in Schilberg, together with a column of Churchill gun tanks, 20 January 1945. (Author's Collection)

Left: XII Corps attack. Troops of the 1st Bn Glasgow Highlanders being carried by tanks of 8th Armd Bde through the damaged village of Hongen. They must be well out of enemy artillery range to be travelling so exposed. 19 January 1945. (IWM - B 13924)

Week 34: 23–29 January 1945

The immediate Allied plan in the northern, 21st Army Group, sector was for a two-pronged attack to clear the area between the Rhine and the Maas from Düsseldorf to Nijmegen, establishing a bridge-head north of the Ruhr. To the south of British Second Army, US Ninth Army would carry out the southern prong of the offensive, but only after US First Army had taken the Roer dams. The British and Canadian attack was code-named Operation 'Veritable', the American, Operation 'Grenade'. The combined assault was planned to start on 8 February.

Before these operations could be launched, however, the area known as the Roermond triangle had to be cleared. This was achieved by 26 January, units of British Second Army's XII Corps in Operation 'Blackcock' pushing the enemy back east of the River Roer everywhere except for a small bridge-head in the area of Vlodrop.

South of 21st Army Group in the Ardennes sector, 12th Army Group (US First and Third Armies) continued their offensive to win back

all the ground taken during the German assault, capturing the area south and south-east of St. Vith and finally eliminating the entire German salient by 28 January, when US First Army troops began their final advance to the Siegfried Line. Initially at least the countryside was just as inhospitable as in the Ardennes, but by attacking through the Eifel the rugged country around Monschau, in which the Roer dams were located, was avoided. General Bradley's forces were able to bypass and outflank the dams, yet were still in a position to support the main effort further north. Bradley intended to attack north-eastwards along the German frontier between Monschau and St. Vith, and to seize the town of Euskirchen, thereby putting US troops behind the main enemy defences. The first phase of the offensive was to be a frontal attack to penetrate the West Wall between Monschau and Leutzkampen, the main effort being made by XVIII Ab Corps on the right wing, fighting through the Losheim Gap (as the Germans had done – albeit in the other direction – in 1914, 1940 and 1944). To their

Above: The crew of this Sherman are having to replace both tracks on their Sherman – not a pleasant job at any time, but one can imagine the difficulties in the depths of winter! Near Wilz, Luxembourg, 26 January 1945. (US Army via Real War Photos - A 887B)

Left: Battle of the Reichswald Forest. British and Canadian troops, massed to enter the Reichswald Forest, part of Operation 'Veritable', the thrust from the Nijmegen bridgehead, which was the beginning of the battle of the Rhineland. Note the leading infantry-covered Sherman is a 17pdr Firefly. Picture taken early February 1945. (IWM - AP 5357)

north, US V Corps would aim to penetrate the western arm of the West Wall in the Monschau Forest. In reserve was US VII Corps, ready to exploit either attack. Ridgway's airborne troops opened their attack on 28 January, V Corps' the following day.

On their right, Patton's Third Army would, in the first phase of operations, protect First Army's right flank, opening its own offensive on 29 January which was also designed to force a way through the Siegfried Line. US VIII Corps on the right flank also began their attack on the 29th. The terrain and foul weather proved every bit as hostile as the enemy; snow everywhere up to 2 feet deep and in places up to waist level not only choked the roads but also hid the enemy's mines, which made progress difficult and dangerous.

Much farther south, French First Army's II Corps launched a new offensive across the River Ill, while, on the 29th, US XXI Corps crossed the Colmar Canal.

Week 35: 30 January–6 February 1945

Roosevelt and Churchill met in Malta on the 30th, prior to the Yalta Conference with Stalin, which began on 4 February. All the Allied armies were making progress on all fronts. On 4 February it was announced that Belgium was now clear of enemy.

In US 12th Army Group's area, the difficult winter conditions slowed XVIII Ab Corps'

progress and it was not until the fifth day of the attack (1 February) that they reached the West Wall. To their north, US V Corps had entered Germany on 31 January as they advanced to take the Schwammenauel dam. Now, however, Eisenhower decided to halt 12th Army Group's drive on Euskirchen and move troops north to Ninth Army's sector. On 30 January, 78th Inf Div (XIX Corps, US Ninth Army) opened their offensive towards the River Ruhr along the northern edge of the Monschau Forest.

On 3 February, Patton ordered Third Army's XII Corps to initiate a night attack on Bitburg on 6/7 February, while VIII Corps continued its drive towards Prüm. It appeared that the Germans were withdrawing panzer units from the Western Front for deployment in the east, leaving their western defences in the hands of low-grade infantry, thousands of whom would eventually surrender or desert.

To the south, US Seventh Army crossed the River Moder on 1 February and advanced towards Oberhofen, while French First Army in Alsace continued to make progress near Colmar, completing its capture by 3 February.

Week 36: 7–13 February 1945

On 8 February near Nijmegen, the British/ Canadian offensive (Operation 'Veritable') began as planned, and the Rhine was reached at Millingen. By 10 February they had reached

Right: The Canadians in Germany. Up at the northern end of the front lines, in the Canadian sector, vehicles of the 3rd Canadian Infantry Brigade travel along the flooded MSR (Main Supply Route) near Cleve, 13 February 1945. (National Archives of Canada - PA 143946)

Kleve and Materborn, capturing Kleve on the 11th.

In US First Army's sector, Schmidt was taken on 7 February. The Germans opened the Schwammenauel dam in an attempt to delay the American advance.

US Third Army continued its attacks near Prüm in the north, while XII Corps troops kept up the pressure in the south. In III Corps' area a limited attack took place across the River Our and the bridge-head was enlarged during the week. In VIII Corps 11th Armd Div captured Habscheid, 4th Inf Div took Brandscheid and Schlausenbach, and 87th Inf Div attacked the Siegfried Line. The armoured divisions in Third Army, and elsewhere, had now begun to receive the new M24 Chaffee light tanks for their cavalry recce squadrons which greatly improved their capabilities. Also, flame-throwers were received by 4th and 6th Armd Divs to fit into their medium tanks. These proved ideal for use against pillboxes. Units of XX Corps launched the night attack as planned, using artificial moonlight (from searchlights) on Saarlautern, Roden and Fraulautern.

Everywhere a sudden thaw had given the engineers even more almost impossible problems with streams becoming raging torrents 100–200 feet wide, the churning water overturning assault boats and floats, drowning many GIs. Another problem was that much of the stacked reserve ammunition toppled and had to be re-stacked. Despite these added difficulties, the assaults continued.

Week 37: 14–20 February 1945

Montgomery's 21st Army Group had reached the south bank of the Rhine opposite Emmerich by the 14th, and in the north three days later the Canadians reached the Rhine on a 10-mile front. British XXX Corps attacked Goch.

US Ninth Army began Operation 'Grenade' on 16 February.

Patton's US Third Army launched new attacks from southern Luxembourg (XII Corps) and Saarlouis (XX Corps), and by the 18th VIII

Left: Warning sign on the German/Dutch border, 14 February 1945. (IWM - PL 390102)

Above: Near Bellendorf, Germany, men of Co 'B' 91st Chemical Bn, 5 US Inf Div, lay down a smoke barrage with their 4.2in mortar, to cover other troops of the division whilst they are crossing the River Sauer. (US Army via Real War Photos - A 2621)

Corps had broken through the Siegfried Line north of Echternach. These advances had created a 'bulge' in the front line (the 'Vianden Bulge'), which then had to be cleared. Prüm was finally taken and the Americans continued to clear pillboxes and strongpoints along the Siegfried Line. US Seventh Army attacked near Saarbrücken.

Week 38: 21–26 February 1945
Goch was taken by XX Corps' 51st Highland Div on the 21st, and two days later US Ninth Army crossed the Roer.

On 23 February, US First and 9th Armies launched a new offensive along the Roer, most particularly in the area of Jülich and Düren. The river was crossed in several places and Düren was taken on the 25th by First Army's VII Corps. Soon more bridge-heads had been secured, in the north and south, and these were rapidly expanded.

US Third Army finally straightened out the 'Vianden Bulge' this week, thanks to the combined efforts of US VIII and XII Corps. The scale of the problem which they had faced can be gauged by the fact that from 29 January to 21 February, VIII Corps units destroyed a staggering 936 enemy-held pillboxes. On the 21st, when 10th Armd Div had reached a point just six miles from Trier, Patton ordered XX Corps to attack and capture this key German communications centre.

Week 39: 27 February–5 March 1945
In 21st Army Group's sector, Udem and Kalkar fell at the beginning of the week, and by 3 March US Ninth Army had linked-up with the Canadians at Geldern.

In US First Army's sector, VII Corps units crossed the River Erft at Modrath and had taken Coblenz, Bonn and Cologne by the 5th; two days later they linked-up with the Canadians.

Above: On the Cleve-Calcar road, Canadians prepare to follow up retreating Germans. Before resuming the advance these 'Kangaroo' crews have a quick 'wash and brush up' in a sea of mud. Their Kangaroo APCs (de-turreted Canadian-built RAM tanks) held 11 infantry soldiers in full battle order, plus a crew of two, 22 February 1945. (Author's Collection)

Left: Infantrymen of 90 Inf Div and AFVs of 6th Armd Div, US Third Army, move through the dragons' teeth of the Siegfried Line, near Heckuschied, Germany, February 1945. (IWM - EA 54147)

Above: A half-track and trailer, belonging to 10th Armd Div, crosses a pontoon bridge over the Saar River, at Taben, in the US Third Army sector on 25 February 1945. (US Army via Real War Photos - A 985)

Right: Men of the Queen's Own Camerons of Winnipeg open a parcel from home in a pup tent-covered German dugout in the Hochwald Forest, Germany, 5 March 1945. (National Archives of Canada - PA 137458)

In US Third Army's sector, all corps were making rapid gains; on the 5th they took their 200,000th prisoner.

Crossing the Rhine

Although by early 1945, the Allied armies had reached the Rhine in both the north (Nijmegen) and the south (Strasbourg), in the centre the German Ardennes offensive had delayed their advance, so it was not until early March that they approached this last great symbolic defensive line along its entire length. The SHAEF master plan called for the crossing to take place in 21st Army Group's area, with assistance from US Ninth Army, plus airborne troops. The assault was planned on a 4-division frontage – two on 21st Army Group's front and two in the attached 9th Army area – the whole supported by an airborne attack mounted by US 17th Ab and British 6th Ab Divs. The area chosen was just to the north of the Ruhr. Detailed, methodical planning was necessary, because it was known that the Germans had some of their best remaining troops holding the line in this area, including paratroops. In preparation for the coming battles, an entire Canadian corps had been brought from Italy, plus a British division from the Middle East. The airborne troops were to be used in a novel way, namely as follow-up forces rather than in advance of any amphibious crossing attempt. The river would be crossed by night, and the airborne troops would be dropped nearby the following morning, to participate in the close tactical battle. In all Montgomery had some 29 divisions under his command, but not all of them would be used in the operation because the Allies' 'long left flank' had still to be defended. Before this setpiece assault could take place, however, the Allies were fortunate enough to 'bounce' crossings over the river elsewhere.

Remagen

The honour of being the first unit to capture a crossing over the great river fell to a detachment of US Ninth Armd Div – of III Corps in General Hodges' US First Army. They reached

Below: Into Cologne. Tanks of the US First Army moving into Germany's third city, on 7 March 1945. They captured over 3,600 prisoners in the battle to take the city. (IWM - EA 55822)

Above: Men of the 11th Inf Regt, 5 Inf Div, US Third Army boarding trucks that will take them even closer to the Rhine in pursuit of the enemy. The photograph also gives an excellent view of the ubiquitous little Jeep, over 630,000 of which were built during the war. One of the Jeeps mounts a cal .30 M1917A1 Browning machine gun on its tripod mounting. It was the standard support machine gun in the US Army. 7 March 1945. (US Army via Real War Photos - A 2641)

Right: A view of the Remagen Bridge, taking in the quad heavy .50 cal machine guns of a Multiple .50in MG Carriage M51, which belonged to 639th AAA Bn, US First Army. (Tank Museum)

Left: Excellent close-up of an 81mm mortar crew of 141 Inf Regt, 36th Inf Div, US Seventh Army, firing a mission. 9 March 1945. (US Army via Real War Photos - A 3197)

Right: Winterberg, Germany. Men of the 11th Inf Regt, 5 Inf Div, move along a country road. Note the various half-tracks and jeeps on either side, plus on the right of the photograph, two HMC M8s, which mounted a 75mm howitzer on a M5 light tank chassis. (US Army via Real War Photos - A2643)

Right: Men of HQ Co, 2nd Bn, 11th Inf Regt, 5 Inf Div, move along the bank of the Moselle River, opposite Maden, Germany, as they advance on Lutz, 15 March 1945. (US Army via Real War Photos - A 2642)

the river opposite the small town of Remagen in the late morning of 7 March and were amazed to find that the double track railway bridge was still intact. Led by Lieutenant Karl Timmerman, a small detachment rushed the bridge. The bridge garrison set off the demolition charges, but amazingly the bridge remained almost completely intact and the GIs quickly chased off the remnant of the defenders, disconnected the charges that had not detonated and proudly reported their amazing success. They were swiftly reinforced and by evening a firm bridge-head had been established. Hitler, who had ordered that no bridges over the Rhine were to be captured on

pain of death, was furious and his immediate reaction was to sack FM von Rundstedt (yet again!), replacing him with FM Kesselring from the Italian Front. Of course this single crossing would clearly not suffice for the entire Allied forces, so other, more substantial crossings were needed both above and below Remagen.

US Third Army Crossings

In early March Remagen was the only crossing-point in Allied hands, and it looked as though the next one would be the setpiece assault which Montgomery had been planning so methodically. Patton, however, had other

Left: Rehearsals for crossing the Rhine. Troops of US Ninth Army paddle small storm boats across the River Maas, whilst larger assault craft await their turn, during amphibious crossing rehearsals. (Author's Collection)

Below: Tucked up a sidestreet, fairly close to the Remagen bridge, the machine gunner on this M3 half-track gets ready to engage any enemy aircraft trying to bomb the bridge. Note also the Browning Automatic Rifle lying beside him. The German engineer commanders at Remagen were executed for not blowing the bridge in time, despite the fact that it was really a fault with the demolition equipment. (US Army via Real War Photos - A 281)

ideas! Bradley had already given him permission to cross the river, and he had been looking into an ingenious plan to get a small body of troops over the river in artillery observation and army liaison aircraft (his army had some 200 of these and each could take a passenger, so in theory an infantry battalion could be got across in about 1½ hours!). However, the light aircraft were never used, because they were not needed. At 2030 hrs on 22 March, the leading assault boats of Co K, 3rd Bn, 11th Inf Regt, 5th Inf Div, crossed at Nierstein without a shot being fired. Further upstream at Oppenheim, Cos A and B, of the 1st Bn of the regiment, crossed at the same time and engaged in a short machine-gun battle. The entire crossing had been achieved with just 20 casualties and Patton was delighted at having put one over on Monty! He informed Bradley immediately, but asked

Right: Dense clouds of white smoke – from white phosphorus smoke shells fired by US Third Army artillery – bursting on the steep east bank of the Rhine, 26 March 1945. (IWM - EA 59960)

him not to make any official announcement so as to avoid possible counter-attacks. During the next morning tanks and tank destroyers were ferried across and by late afternoon on the 23rd, a Class 40 treadway bridge had been completed at Nierstein. Patton was unable to contain himself for very long and just hours before the main 21st Army Group crossing was due to begin he 'phoned Bradley again: 'Brad,' he shouted. "For God's sake tell the world

we're across ... I want the world to know that Third Army made it before Monty starts across!'[1]

Operation 'Plunder'

Despite US Third Army's success, the main assault, by 21st Army Group, was launched on a 25-mile front between Emmerich and Rheinberg. Troops, vehicles and equipment were concentrated behind an almost continuous

Right: Crossing at St Goar. Infantrymen of 354 Inf Regt, 89th Div, US Third Army, crossing the Rhine in their assault boats towards St Goarhausen on the east bank. (IWM - EA 64607)

smoke-screen which lasted throughout the 23rd. The smoke-dischargers were switched off at about 1730 hrs and half an hour later the entire artillery of British Second and US Ninth Armies opened fire and continued to pour in shells and rockets until 0945 hrs next day. H-Hour for the leading amphibian-borne troops was 2100 hrs on 23 March, four battalions of XXX Corps (51 Highland Div plus a Canadian Bde) crossing the river in seven minutes, using 150 Buffalo tracked amphibians. The enemy contested the landing and there was a fierce battle in the area around Rees, where the casualties included the GOC, Major-General Thomas Rennie, who was killed. The riverside town was not cleared until the morning of 26 March, by troops of 3rd Canadian Inf Div, and it took four more days to clear Emmerich. Everyone was surprised by the tenacity of the Germans, who were fighting more fiercely than at any time since Normandy. 'It says a lot for the morale of those German parachute and panzer troops,' commented XXX Corps commander, Lieutenant-General Sir Brian Horrocks, 'that with chaos, disorganisation and disillusion all around them they should still be resisting so stubbornly.' On the far right of XII Corps' sector, 1st Cdo Bde crossed almost undetected and infiltrated into the outskirts of Wesel, just before some 200 RAF Lancasters 'neutralised' the town. Around Xanten, 15th (Scottish) Div spearheaded XII Corps' assault of the eastern bank.

Meanwhile, at Rheinberg, south of Wesel at 0200 hrs on 24 March, 30th and 79th US Inf Divs of US Ninth Army's XVI Corps, crossed with minimal opposition, achieving all their objectives without any major problems. Indeed by dusk that day they had constructed a 1,150-foot 'treadway' bridge. Altogether, twelve bridges were in service across the Rhine by the evening of 26 March.

Operation 'Varsity'

The airborne assault went in at 1000 hrs 24 March, the drop zone being around Hamminkeln, some seven miles east of the Rhine. One of the tasks allocated to the airborne troops was to capture intact some of the bridges over the Ijssel which flows parallel

to the Rhine between Wesel and Emmerich. There were considerable casualties from enemy AA fire, despite pre-drop airstrikes and softening up by accompanying fighter-bombers. 'Varsity' was destined to be the last ever action by glider-borne troops.

British Prime Minister Winston Churchill had been present throughout the crossing operations and later crossed in a Buffalo to the Wesel bridgehead.

Field Marshal Montgomery, who considered Operation 'Plunder' to be one of his best-organised operations, summed it up later in just sixteen words: 'Our attack across the

Above: Crossing at St Goar. Troops of US Third Army raising the Stars and Stripes at the Lorelei Rock overlooking the Rhine Gorge, close to St Goar, where 354 Inf Regt had made their crossing. (US Army)

Above: Operation 'Varsity'. This photograph shows the great air armada on its way towards the Rhine. Dakotas of the British airborne fleet are the ones flying in formation, after meeting the American fleet over Wavre in Belgium, whilst high above them are Stirlings towing gliders – an aerial crossroads but not a traffic jam! The photo was taken on 24 March, H hour on the DZ was 1000hrs, the DZ being some miles east of the river. It was the first phase of Operation 'Plunder' and was completely successful. (Bruce Roberston)

Right: US paratroopers of 17th US Ab Div take cover in the orchard in which they have dropped. Their initial objective is the farm building in the rear of the photograph, a German strongpoint, which must be taken quickly. In all the 17th Ab Div took 2,000 prisoners and the Br 6th Ab Div, a further 1,500. (IWM -

Above: American paratroopers dig in within their DZ, some miles east of the Rhine near Hamminkeln. All airborne troops were on the ground by 1230hrs and in a matter of hours both American and British had seized all their objectives assigned for Day 1. Link-up was made with British ground troops by nightfall. (IWM - KY 60486)

Left: Follow-up to the crossing at Wesel. Landing 1 Cheshires on the afternoon of 24 March, to support 1st Cdo Bde of 2nd Br Army, at Wesel. Photograph shows two Buffaloes dropping their cargoes on the east bank. The damaged railway bridge can be seen behind them. (IWM - BU 2335)

Above: Crossing at Frankenthal. It was at 0230hrs on the 26th that men of the 3rd Inf Div, US Seventh Army, crossed in assault boats with outboard motors as seen here on the west bank. (IWM - EA 59875)

Right: US Third Army engineers of 80th Inf Div built this 1,865ft long 'Sunday Punch' pontoon treadway bridge at Mainz. (IWM - EA 80873)

Rhine, supported by a very large-scale airborne operation, was an outstanding success.'

In all there were 23 assault crossings of the River Rhine, the last five being well to the south in French First Army's sector:

1. 7 March, 1600 hrs: Remagen, US First Army, 27 Armd Inf Bn
2. 22 March, 2200 hrs: Oppenheim, US Third Army, 11th Inf Regt
3. 22 March, 2200 hrs: Nierstein, US Third Army, 11th Inf Regt
4. 23 March, 2100 hrs: Rees, British Second Army, 51st Highland Div
5. 23 March, 2200 hrs: Wesel, British Second Army, 1st Cdo Bde
6. 24 March, 0200 hrs: Büderich, US Ninth Army, 119th Inf Regt
7. 24 March, 0200 hrs: Wallach, US Ninth Army, 117th Inf Regt
8. 24 March, 0200 hrs: Rheinberg, US Ninth Army, 120th Inf Regt
9. 24 March, 0200 hrs: Xanten, British Second Army, 15th Scottish Div
10. 24 March, 0300 hrs: Walsum, US Ninth Army, 315th Inf Regt

11. 24 March, 0300 hrs: Orsoy, US Ninth Army, 313th Inf Regt
12. 25 March, 0001 hrs: Boppard, US Third Army, 345th Inf Regt
13. 25 March, 0001 hrs: Rhens, US Third Army, 347th Inf Regt
14. 26 March, 0200 hrs: St Goar, US Third Army, 354th Inf Regt
15. 26 March, 0200 hrs: Oberwesel, US Third Army, 353rd Inf Regt
16. 26 March, 0200 hrs: Hamm, US Seventh Army, 45th Inf Div
17. 26 March, 0230 hrs: Frankenthal, US Seventh Army, 3rd Inf Div
18. 28 March, 0100 hrs: Mainz, US Third Army, 317th Inf Regt
19. 31 March, 0230 hrs: Speyer, French First Army, 3rd Regt Tirailleurs Algériens
20. 31 March, 0600 hrs: Germersheim, French First Army, 4th Regt Tirailleurs Algériens
21. 31 March, 0600 hrs: Mechtersheim, French First Army, 151st Inf Div
22. 2 April: Leimersheim, French First Army, 9th Colonial Inf Div
23. 15 April, 1100 hrs, French First Army, 23rd Inf Regt

Above: This trio of British soldiers in Geilenkirchen near Munchengladbach provide good shots of two varieties of Sten Guns – the shiny Sten on the left is a Mk 5, whilst the other carried by the middle soldier is probably a Mk 2. In addition, the main weapon of the trio is the PIAT (Projector Infantry Anti-Tank) hanging over his shoulder. The PIAT had a combat range of only 100 yards, but could fire smoke and HE rounds to far greater ranges. (IWM - BU 1335)

Above: Machine gunners of 303rd Inf Regt, 97th Inf Div, US First Army, cover an important intersection in Siegburg – east of the Rhine and north-east of Bonn, with their .30cal M1917A1 Browning Machine Gun, 10 April 1945. (US Army via Real War Photos - A 4185)

Right: Sherman crews belonging to A Sqn SHQ 1st Lothian and Border Horse, relaxing after the eventual capture of Arnhem, on 12 April 1945. Note how both Shermans have additional track plates on the sides of their hulls and turrets, in order to give 'The Ronson Lighter' (as the Sherman was called because it was: 'guaranteed to light first time') extra protection. (Author's Collection)

With this last major obstacle behind them, the Allied armies could now press on into the enemy heartland.

Notes

1. Third Army's official announcement read: 'Without the benefit of aerial bombardment, ground smoke, artillery preparation or airborne assistance [all digs at 21st Army Group!], the Third Army at 2200hrs, Thursday evening, 22 March, crossed the Rhine River.'

11
Into Germany

The Last Few Weeks

On 26 March 1945, General Miles Dempsey, CinC British Second Army told his troops: 'This is collapse! The German line is broken. The enemy no longer has a coherent system of defence between the Rhine and the Elbe. It is difficult to see what there is to stop us now.' His enthusiasm was undoubtedly shared by all the Allied commanders, but there were still some 45 days to go before the Germans surrendered, so there was still plenty of fighting to be done.

General Eisenhower was about to modify his plans, in line with what had been agreed with the Soviets, namely that the main attack from the west would be directed from the Kassel area, directly eastwards towards Leipzig, through what remained of the Germans'

industrial heartland, rather than at Berlin which the Russians were rapidly approaching. At the same time, 21st Army Group, supported by US Ninth Army, would clear out the whole area from Kiel and Lübeck westwards. In the south he would also endeavour to link-up with the Russians in the Danube valley, by thrusting south-eastwards, so as to prevent the establishing of a Nazi redoubt in southern Germany. This plan did not have entire immediate Allied approval; Churchill, for example, was still advocating that a major attempt be made to reach Berlin before the Russians.

Eisenhower had at his command nearly 4½ million men, including ninety active divisions (twenty-five of which were armoured and five airborne: sixty-one American, twelve British, eleven French, five Canadian and one Polish).

Below: Excellent photograph of a US Third Army 40mm Bofors LAA gun outside the Opera House in Frankfurt, 27 March 1945. (US Army via Real War Photos - A 262)

When the drive began Montgomery's 21st Army Group controlled thirty divisions, which included the twelve US divisions in US Ninth Army, together with the newly arrived Canadian corps from Italy. Bradley had thirty-four divisions, including six in his new army, General Gerow's Fifteenth Army, which was intended to be a mainly occupying force, initially with rear echelon assignments although they were made responsible for 66th Inf Div which were currently containing the besieged Brittany ports of Lorient and St-Nazaire. General Devers' 6th Army Group had twelve US and eleven French divisions, two of the latter being employed in other areas – one on the Alpine front facing Italy, the other on the Gironde estuary in south-west France.

Week 43: 27 March–2 April 1945

To the north of 21st Army Group's area, Canadian First Army's main tasks were to open a supply route through Arnhem, advance northwards to clear the rest of the coastal area of Holland, then to continue on across the Ems towards Wilhelmshaven and Oldenburg. Canadian II Corps initially met strong resis-

tance in its advance towards Emmerich but captured the town on the 29th, then extended their bridge-head, while on their left, Can I Corps began its advance on Arnhem. In British Second Army's area, leading troops of XXX Corps reached Ijsselburg on the River Ijssel on 27 March, and XVIII Ab Corps advanced through the Wesel Forest. On 30 March this formation ceased to be operational, prior to coming under command of US Ninth Army, and British 6th Ab Div passed to VIII Corps. The main intended advances of the three corps in General Dempsey's army were to be: in the north, XXX Corps, targeted on Enschede, Bremen and Hamburg; in the centre, XII Corps on Rheine, Nienburg and Lunëburg; on the right VIII Corps on Osnabrück, Celle and Ulzen. By 2 April, XII Corps had reached the Dortmund–Ems Canal at Rheine, and VIII Corps was continuing its advance on Osnabrück.

South of the British, in US Ninth Army's sector, XVI Corps was advancing into the Ruhr where a major pocket of resistance was being established. By 1 April, US Ninth and First Armies had joined-up at Lippstadt thereby

Below: 7th Armd Div, Br Second Army. A column of Armoured Personnel Carriers (APCs) containing men of 9 DLI, near Borken, wait before moving north to take Weseke. 28 March 1945. (IWM - BU 2846)

Left: A 7th Armd Div Cromwell passing through the badly damaged small town of Borken, in their drive east of the Rhine. 30 March 1945. (IWM - BU 2895)

closing a ring around the Ruhr and trapping the whole of Field Marshal Model's Army Group B plus part of Army Group H. The enemy pocket was some 70 miles long and 50 miles wide. XIX Corps units reached the Cologne–Berlin autobahn, while XVI Corps advanced in the sector south of Haltern. On the 2nd, XIII Corps took Münster and pushed on towards the Weser, while XIX Corps was fighting in the Teutoburger Wald and XVI Corps reached the Dortmund–Ems canal.

On 28 March in US First Army's sector, VII, III and V Corps reached the River Lahn, and US First and Third Armies linked-up on the Cologne–Frankfurt autobahn north of Idstein, trapping many enemy troops in the Wiesbaden–Bingen area. On the 29th III Corps started their offensive towards the Eder which they reached next day, as did V Corps. By 31 March VII Corps' 3rd Armd Div were fighting for Paderborn which they captured on 1 April.

At the beginning of the week, VIII Corps of Patton's Third Army widened and strengthened its bridge-head across the Rhine, in the area of Wiesbaden, while farther south XX Corps prepared to cross both the Rhine and the Main in the Mainz area – they had established a secure bridge-head at Mainz on the 28th. The enemy could do little to halt Patton's armoured columns. Frankfurt was captured on 29 March and XX Corps pushed northwards in the direction of Kassel, reaching the Eder on the 30th, while XII Corps was advancing in the Hersfeld sector, near Hanau. Enemy resistance appeared to be hardening in the area between Fulda and the line of the Rivers Werra and Weser.

South of them, US Seventh Army had also reached the Main by the 28th, in the area of Obernau where XV Corps established a bridge-head, while 44th Inf Div of the same corps

Left: A mixture of tanks and other vehicles belonging to 7th Armd Div are seen here in the relatively undamaged village of Ahaus, north-west of Münster, Westphalia, 30 March 1945. (IWM - BU 3135)

crossed the Neckar that day, making for Mannheim which they entered on the 29th. US XV Corps was then held up around Aschaffenburg, but XXI Corps continued on northeastwards towards Würzburg and Königshofen, while VI Corps advanced along the Neckar valley to make contact with French Fist Army on 1 April.

In the south, French First Army made final preparations for its offensive across the Rhine in the Germersheim area, which it opened on 31 March and soon widened to reach Linkenheim, having cut the Karlsruhe–Frankfurt road near Mingolsheim and Bruchsal.

Surrender

On 31 March, General Eisenhower issued a proclamation to the German troops and people, urging the former to surrender and the latter to begin planting crops. He described their hopeless situation and explained how further resistance would only add to their miseries in the future. 'My purpose was to bring the whole bloody business to an end,' he wrote later. Sadly, however, such was the hold that Hitler and his gang had on the German people, via the Gestapo and SS, that they stubbornly continued to fight.

Week 44: 3–9 April 1945

On the northern flank Canadian II Corps, which had been advancing north-eastwards towards Oldenburg, crossed the River Ems in the Mappen–Lathen area on 8 April

On 3 April the leading elements of British Second Army reached the Dortmund–Ems Canal around Lingen and established a bridgehead there (XXX Corps) and also at Rheine (XII Corps) on 4 April. Leading elements of VIII Corps entered Osnabrück the same day, while others pushed on towards Minden, establishing a bridge-head over the Weser in the Minden–Stolzenau area on the 7th, then pushing on south-eastwards from Nienburg towards the River Leine which they reached on 8 April. Meanwhile to their north, XXX Corps had taken enemy defensive positions east of Lingen and was pressing on towards Bremen.

In US Ninth Army's sector, having completed the capture of Münster XIII Corps moved up to

the Weser and established a bridge-head on the 7th, while farther south XIX Corps began to exert pressure on the Germans trapped in the Ruhr pocket. US First Army also began its operation against the Ruhr pocket on 3 April with III Corps and XVIII Ab Corps, the former between the Rivers Leine and Ruhr, the latter between the Ruhr and the Rhine. Pressure was continued, XVIII Ab Corps opening an offensive at the confluence of the Ruhr and Rhine on the 6th. That same day, V Corps reached the Weser, as did VII Corps on the 7th, but they found that all the bridges over the river in their sector had been destroyed.

On 8 April, XIII Corps' 5th Armd Div was ordered to cross the Leine, south of Hanover. On the 9th, units of XIII Corps launched assaults on Hanover from the north, northwest and west.

In US First Army's sector, XVIII Corps troops crossed the River Sieg in the Ruhr pocket, while VII Corps established a strong bridgehead over the Weser; V Corps, already across

by the 8th, was advancing eastwards. All corps continued to advance towards the Elbe, VII Corps making for Nordhausen and the River Leine in the Göttingen area.

On 2 April, in US Third Army area, 4th Armd Div established a crossing over the River Werra, then advanced to Stregda and Goldbach, while 11th Armd Div did the same at Ritschenhausen, then advanced fifteen miles. In XX Corps' zone, Kassel was captured on 4 April by 80th Inf Div, while 6th Armd Div crossed the Wehre and advanced 20 miles closely followed by 65th Inf Div. US Third Army continued to advance rapidly with XX Corps north, VIII Corps centre and XII south. Only around Kassel in the north did the enemy make a determined stand, even after the city had fallen.

On 3 April, in US Seventh Army's sector Aschaffenburg surrendered to XV Corps' 45th Inf Div after three days of savage fighting. US XXI Corps attacked Würzburg and established a bridge-head over the River Main in the

Above: Soldiers of 44th Armd Inf Bn, 6th Armd Div, US Third Army, dodge enemy fire during street fighting in Oberdoria, Germany, 4th April 1945. (US Army)

Above: Ohrdurf, 4 April 1945. Gen Eisenhower and a party of high-ranking US Army officers looking at the bodies of Russian and Polish prisoners, shot by their SS guards, before they retreated in front of 4th Armd Div, US Third Army. Gens Bradley and Patton can also be seen in the group. (US Army)

western end of the town. By 7 April XV Corps had taken Neustadt on the River Saal. They continued the attack, with XV Corps advancing on the Hohe Rhon hills, while XXI and V Corps advanced towards Schweinfurt and Heilbronn.

To their south, French First Army extended its bridge-head and captured Karlsruhe on the 3rd, then prepared to occupy the Black Forest, moving south-westwards towards Freiburg and south-eastwards towards Tübingen. Leading elements of French II Corps reached the River Neckar in the vicinity of Laufen, the River Enz at Mühlacker, the outskirts of Pforzheim and captured Stein and Königsbach. On 8 April French 1st Inf Div took Pforzheim, Dieten-hausen and Dietingen, and established a bridge-head on the River Enz near Mühlhausen.

Week 45: 10–16 April 1945

In the north, Canadian II Corps had advanced towards Groningen and Oldenburg, taking the

former town on the 16th; Canadian I Corps had attacked Arnhem on the 12th and taken it on the 15th.

South of them, Second Army's XXX Corps was pushing on towards Bremen while XII Corps made for Soltau and VIII Corps for Celle, crossing the Leine near Westen and the Aller at Celle on the 11th, then pressing on towards Uelzen. By the end of the week XXX Corps was close to Bremen, and VIII Corps was encountering strong resistance at Uelzen.

On 10 April in US Ninth Army's sector, XIII Corps took Hanover and pushed on south of the city to Pattensen on the River Leine; XVI Corps reached Essen, Bochum and Gelsenkirchen on the same day. In US XIX Corps' sector, 2nd Armd Div, which was providing advance guards for XIX Corps, made a spectacular leap forward to reach the Elbe near Magdeburg on the 11th. On the 12th XIII Corps also reached the river further north near Wittenberg, whilst XIX Corps established a bridge-head over the river near Randau, south

of Magdeburg. Meanwhile XVI Corps had advanced into the Ruhr pocket, reaching the River Ruhr opposite Witten on the 11th, then taking the northern sector between Witten and Westhofen and completing the capture of Dortmund on the 13th. On the 15th, XIII Corps launched an offensive along the River Saale, aiming to take the high ground between the Saale and the Rhine. In US First Army's area, XVIII Ab Corps crossed the River Sieg into the Ruhr pocket, in pursuit of the enemy who were beginning to retire from their defensive positions. By 14 April XVIII Ab Corps had begun the final phase of their operation; opposition was crumbling and by the 16th they had taken more than 20,000 prisoners. US III Corps had been attacking the same objective and by the 14th had secured the area between the Rivers Ruhr and Honne. US VII Corps advanced towards Nordhausen, which they

took on the 11th, as well as Osterode, Tettenborn and Neuhof, then continued north-eastwards towards the Rivers Elbe and Mulde. US V Corps reached the bridges over the River Mulde between Colditz and Lastau on the 15th, and by the 16th both VII and V Corps had bridge-heads across the river and 9th Armd Div (V Corps) had entered Colditz.

US Third Army was also pushing the enemy towards the River Mulde. At Coburg the armour cut loose on the 11th, bypassing Erfurt, Weimar, Jena and Gera, crossing the Mulde and continuing on for some 80 miles, halting at Chemnitz. The bypassed towns fell to the follow-up infantry. On the 14th Patton opened the Roosevelt Memorial Railway Bridge over the Rhine, two days after the President's death. On the 15th, 120th Evacuation Hospital moved to Ettersburg to provide medical services for Buchenwald where

Left: The commander of a M5A1 light tank belonging to the 5th Armd Div, US Ninth Army, uses a portable loudspeaker to tell the citizens of Peine, that their Burgermeister (Mayor) has surrendered the town, and that they must hand in all weapons and stay off the streets. 10 April 1945. (US Army via Real War Photos - A 881B)

Below: A column of tanks and half-tracks belonging to 5th Armd Div, US Ninth Army, stops for a short break in open country between woods, during their advance to Bismarck, north of Magdeburg, 11 April 1945. (US Army via Real War Photos - A 881A)

120,000 of the Nazis' victims needed immediate care.

In US Seventh Army's sector, XXI Corps was advancing towards Schweinfurt and along the east bank of the Rhine. XV Corps had been pressing on rapidly south of Nuremburg, reaching Bamberg on the 12th and entering the town the following day, though it was not cleared of enemy until the 14th. After nine days of hard fighting VI Corps troops took Heilbronn, and XV Corps reached Nuremburg on the 16th.

By 12 April, French First Army had established a bridge-head across the River Enz, and I Corps crossed the Rhine north of Kehl on the 15th, while II Corps occupied the Black Forest area.

Week 46: 17–23 April 1945

On the 18th, Canadian I Corps reached the Zuider Zee, isolating enemy forces and virtually ending their offensive operations. They eventually closed along the line of the Rivers Grebbe and Eem where they remained for the remainder of the war. Canadian II Corps area was also virtually clear except for some opposition south-west of Oldenburg.

On 17 April British Second Army's XXX Corps were still fighting in the suburbs of Bremen; XII Corps took Soltau the same day, then advanced swiftly northwards to cut the Bremen–Hamburg autobahn the following day. VIII Corps reached the Elbe in the Lauenburg area the same day, taking Uelzen and Lüneburg on the 18th; 11th Armd Div and 5th Inf Div were concentrating just east of Osnabrück, ready to advance to the Baltic. By the 23rd, XII Corps had reached the Elbe, opposite Hamburg.

In US Ninth Army's area, XIX Corps began an assault on Magdeburg on the 17th.

In US First Army's area, XVIII Corps in the Ruhr pocket took Duisburg, Solingen, Düsseldorf and Werden. By the 18th they were finishing off the remnants of organised resistance. Estimates of prisoners taken in the pocket were a staggering 325,000, more than twice as many as had been expected. Their

Above: Keppel, Austria. A large amount of firepower from carbines, machine guns and main tank guns is directed at the town of Keppel by men of 11th Armd Div, US Third Army. (US Army via Real War Photos - A 614)

Left: Ferrying a Canadian tank across the Ijessel River, near Deventer, Holland, 12 April 1945. This was during the First Canadian Army's clearance of western Holland, as they pressed forward towards Leeuwarden and Groningen. (National Archives of Canada - PA 142407)

Right: Mopping up operations along the Oranje Canal, 12 April 1945. Men of the South Saskatchewan Regiment deal with scattered enemy resistance from positions along the canal bank. (National Archives of Canada - PA 145977)

Right: Advancing towards Groningen to complete the clearance of the west of Holland. A Sherman Firefly belonging to B Squadron Fort Garry Horse carries infantrymen of the Royal Hamilton Light Infantry, during the advance, 13 April 1945. (National Archives of Canada - PA 130935)

Right: Another Sherman belonging to the Fort Garry Horse passes a column of German prisoners, on the way towards Groningen. (National Archives of Canada - PA 130923)

commander, Field Marshal Model, committed suicide on the 21st. III Corps was warned that it was to be transferred to US Third Army shortly, while VII Corps consolidated its positions between the Rivers Elbe and Mulde, taking Halle on the 18th. US V Corps' leading troops (2nd and 9th Inf Divs) converged on Leipzig on the 17th, then launched a co-ordinated attack and captured the city next day. On 21 April VII Corps began an offensive against Dessau, and had taken the entire sector by the 23rd.

On the 17th US Third Army was ordered to change the direction of advance to the south-east into Bavaria to attack the so-called 'German–Austrian Redoubt', while maintaining patrols along the Czech border. This led to VIII Corps being put under command of US First Army; III Corps took its place, but was moved to the southern flank, to be responsible for what had been part of the US Seventh Army's sector. This re-organisation and redeployment took from 17 to 22 April and the assault was then resumed on all fronts. Grafenwöhr was taken by XII Corps, and Pegnitz, south of Bayreuth, by XX Corps. It was soon clear that the enemy defences were merely a

Above: GIs of the 61st Armd Inf Bn ride on the back of a Sherman belonging to 21st Tank Bn, CCA, 10th Armd Div, US Seventh Army, as they move forward towards Bubenorbic, 17 April 1945. (US Army via Real War Photos - A 985B)

Left: Belsen Concentration Camp. When the British liberated the Bergen-Belsen camp near Celle, on 15 April 1945, they found unspeakable horrors, some of which were described on the hastily erected signboard. (Ground Photo Recce Unit, HQ 2nd Army)

Right: 11th Armd Div reaches the Baltic coast, 3 May 1945. Having pushed on from Lubeck, via the autobahn to the coastal town of Travemunde, where they captured the airfield intact and also took a great number of prisoners, the division halted. This Cromwell tank, near the harbour, mounts a 95mm howitzer in place of the usual 6pdr or 75mm gun and was the close support variant. (IWM - BU 5278)

Right: Link-up with the Red Army. British troops of 6th Airborne Division link up with Red Army soldiers near Wismar on the Baltic coast, exchanging handshakes, drinks and cigarettes. (IWM - BU 5230)

thin crust, easily penetrated and the speed of advance gained momentum every day.

In US Seventh Army's sector, XV Corps began its battle for Nuremburg on the 17th; next day XXI Corps troops entered Fürth just west of the city and closed off all exit routes. The city fell on the 20th under the co-ordinated attacks of three infantry divisions of XV Corps (3rd, 42nd and 45th). On the 22nd XXI Corps units reached the Danube at Lauingen and Dillengen, quickly establishing bridgeheads, while further south the river was reached and crossed by VI Corps at Ehringen.

In the south, French First Army's II Corps took Freudenstadt on the 17th and pushed on towards Stuttgart, while I Corps occupied the western part of the Black Forest, reaching Biberach and Mahlberg. On the 20th Stuttgart was attacked by French II Corps and US Seventh Army's VI Corps. Next day French II Corps' 5th Armd Div penetrated the defences and occupied the city.

Week 47: 24–30 April 1945

On the 24th, British XXX Corps launched an offensive against Bremen and completed its capture on the 26th; VIII Corps reached the Elbe at Lauenburg, and XII Corps was now deployed along the west bank of the river opposite Hamburg. The plan was for VIII Corps to assault and establish a bridge-head, while to their right in US Ninth Army's sector, XVIII Corps would establish another bridge-head; VIII Corps would then move troops across with all speed, and turn northwards to take Lübeck, while XII Corps masked off Hamburg (which would surrender unconditionally on 3 May). This last operation began in the early hours of the 29th, 15th Inf Div, supported by 1 Cdo Bde, crossing in amphibians, as in the Rhine crossing, supported by DD tanks. All went according to plan. British XVIII Corps also began its advance towards the Baltic. North of the Elbe the countryside was packed with refugees – military and civilian – fleeing from the armies that were converging from west and east.

In US Ninth Army's sector, all its three corps – XIII, XIX and XVI – were across the Elbe and had dug in on the eastern bank by the end of April.

In US Third Army's area, III Corps had now taken over the former XV Corps' zone and was advancing with three divisions abreast; XII Corps' units were moving south in a long continuous column along the Czech border, XX Corps in the centre with 80th Inf Div (SHAEF reserve) to the rear. III Corps crossed the Altmuhl in three places on the 24th, advanced some 25 miles and captured numerous small towns, while other units reached the Danube. On the 28th another order from 12th Army Group directed Third Army to continue its drive to join the Russians in the Danube valley and to seize Salzburg, US First Army having taken over responsibility for the Czech border. Advancing from their bridge-heads over the Danube, III and XX Corps swept south to reach the Istar on the 29th, while armoured elements of XII Corps had also crossed the Austrian border and were well inside, with enemy resistance collapsing everywhere.

US Seventh Army also pressed on towards the Danube, VI Corps taking Ulm on the 24th, XV Corps Munich on the 30th, while XXI and VI Corps advanced towards the Austrian border in the areas of Garmisch and Rosen-

Above: Tanks of 10th Armd Div, US Seventh Army, entering the famous winter-sports centre of Garmisch-partenkirchen in the Bavarian Alps, 30 April 1945. They halted here to allow 44th and 103rd Inf Divs to pass through their lines and finished the war at Innsbruck on 7 May 1945. (US Army)

heim. By the end of April, XV Corps were mopping-up around Munich while VI Corps was advancing towards Innsbruck and Imst.

On the 24th French First Army's II Corps reached the Swiss frontier at Basel, and I Corps was engaged against a last desperate attempt by German forces to escape into the Bavarian Alps. By the end of April the French Army had crossed the Austrian frontier and occupied Bregenz.

Unconditional Surrender

During the next few days the Germans' situation on all fronts was one of complete collapse. It was soon evident that there had been a total breakdown of any central control, individual units, divisions, corps and armies all surrendering piecemeal to whichever Allied forces were nearest and prepared to accept their surrender. All the time there was a desperate move by both civilians and servicemen to move westwards, out of the clutches of the advancing Red Army. There was only one way to resolve the chaotic situation and that was clearly unconditional surrender by the entire German nation.

12
Victory

Weeks 48 and 49: 1–13 May 1945

There was a series of surrenders by the German forces in North West Europe, the first being triggered by the capitulation in Italy on 2 May 1945. This placed the German forces (mainly Army Group G) just to the north of Italy, in an impossible position and on 2 May their commander, General der Infanterie Friedrich Schulz, sent word asking to whom he should surrender. He was told to apply to General Jacob Devers, commander of 6th Army Group,

the southernmost of SHAEF's army groups. However, he was also told that only unconditional surrender would be acceptable. These German forces therefore capitulated and the surrender document was signed at 1400 hrs on 5 May, the surrender being made effective from noon on the 6th.

Considerably farther north, in the Hamburg area, the local German commander also appreciated the situation and realised that the end was nigh. On 29 April, word came via Stockholm, that Field Marshal Ernest Busch, CinC in the North West, who was then stationed in Norway, and General Georg Lindemann, who was commanding in Denmark, both wished to surrender as soon as the Allied advance reached the Baltic. They did not want to capitulate to the Red Army nor to be ordered to continue to fight by the Nazi hierarchy, so they planned that as soon as 21st Army Group arrived in the Lübeck area, thus cutting them off from the rest of Germany, they would act on their own and immediately capitulate. Montgomery's forces arrived there on 3 May, but because Hitler had committed suicide on 30 April, there was now a new leader of the Third Reich, namely Admiral Karl Dönitz, and he sensibly directed that all German forces everywhere should surrender to the Western Allies. Thus it was that on 3 May 1945, nearly one million German troops, the entire force which had been occupying north-west Germany, Holland, Norway and Denmark, decided to surrender unconditionally to Field Marshal Montgomery. Next day, 4 May, German delegates attended Montgomery's HQ on Lüneburg Heath, to hear the unconditional surrender terms. Admiral Hans von Friedburg, now CinC German Navy, who would later commit suicide, signed the terms, which were to become effective on the morning of 5 May.

Left: Field Marshal Sir Bernard Montgomery with the German delegation led by General-Admiral von Friedburg, outside the tent in which the surrender of all German forces in Denmark, north-west Germany and the Netherlands, will be signed. The location was on Luneburg Heath, some 25 miles south of Hamburg and the date was 4 May 1945. (IWM BU 5142)

Left: Germans on the British front capitulate. Around the table from L to R are: Kontur Adml Wagner, Gen Adml von Friedburg, FM Montgomery, Gen of Inf Kinzel and Col Poleck. Montgomery is seen reading the surrender terms to the German delegates. (IWM - BU 5207)

Left: Gen-Admiral von Friedburg committed suicide soon after signing the surrender docment at Montgomery's tent on Lüneburg Heath. (IWM - BU 6681)

Above: The 'Master Race' is vanquished. Close-up of a group of German prisoners from the Nijmegen area, queuing for food. (Author's Collection)

Right: 'Defeat and humiliation to the Hun' – that is how the original caption to this photograph reads, which shows some of the thousands of prisoners now stumbling through vast stockades for counting. (IWM - FRA 100319)

Above: Reichsmarshall Hermann Goering surrendered to 36 US Inf Div near Mautendorf on 8 May 1945. He is seen here talking to CG 36 Div – Maj Gen John E. Dahlquist and his deputy, Brig Gen Robert I. Stack. Goering was the senior Nazi tried at Nuremburg, but took poison on 15 October 1946, the day before he was due to be hanged. (US Army via Real War Photos - A 3212)

Left: Field Marshal von Rundstedt was also captured by the US 36th Inf Div, Seventh Army and is seen here with his son Lt Hans von Rundstedt and a German medical attendant. He was receiving treatment for arthritis at Bad Tolz, when captured on 2 May 1945. (IWM - EA 65353)

It seemed to General Eisenhower as though the Germans were stalling for time, so as to allow the maximum number of their beaten troops to move westwards into Allied lines and away from the Red Army. He told his Chief of Staff, Lieutenant General W. Bedell Smith, to warn Jodl that unless he stopped prevaricating, the frontier would be closed to prevent any more refugees reaching the West. Finally the German representatives sent a message to Dönitz, asking for authority to make a complete surrender which they wanted to be effective 48 hours after signing. But this could clearly lead to even more delay, so Eisenhower put his foot firmly down and told them that the surrender would be effective 48 hours from midnight of that very day! In the War Room of the SHAEF HQ (in a boys' red brick school in Rheims) Bedell Smith and Jodl signed the unconditional surrender document at 0241 hrs on Monday, 7 May 1945, which was witnessed by the British, French and Russian representatives. All hostilities would therefore officially cease at midnight on Tuesday, 8 May 1945. President Harry S. Truman and Prime Minister Winston Churchill made this historic announcement to both nations on the 8th.

In the early hours of the morning of 8 May 1945, Field Marshal Wilhelm Keitel (Chief of OKW) signed the third and final surrender document in the Berlin suburb of Karlshorst. He was accompanied by Admiral von Friedburg and General Stumpf of the Luftwaffe. At midnight the Germans had been brought into a room draped with the American, British, French and Soviet Union flags. Keitel was asked by Air Chief Marshal Sir Arthur Tedder if he clearly understood what he was signing. When he replied that he did, he, Friedburg and Stumpf all signed, followed by the Allied signatories who were: Marshal Zhukov for the Soviet Union High Command and Air Chief Marshal Tedder, for the Allied Expeditionary Force. Lieutenant General Carl A. Spaatz, Commander US Strategic Air Forces and General de Lattre de Tassigny, Commander of French First Army, also signed as witnesses.

Victory in Europe (VE) Day was thus held on Wednesday, 9 May 1945.

Above: Gen Jean-Marie Lattre de Tassigny represented France at the formal German surrender in the early hours of 8 May 1945, in the Berlin suburb of Karlshorst, signing as a witness. He was then commanding the French First Army, but went on postwar to become the French CGS. (IWM - AP 69738)

It was also on 5 May that a representative of Admiral Dönitz contacted General Eisenhower's SHAEF headquarters at Rheims and proposed surrender, at the same time advising them that all U-boats had been ordered to return to port. General Eisenhower immediately appraised the Soviets of the situation and requested that they send a representative to be present at any negotiations – Major-General Ivan Susloparov, who had long been the Soviets' liaison officer at SHAEF was so designated. Admiral Friedburg arrived at Rheims that day, to be followed rapidly by General Alfred Jodl, Chief of Staff OKW, direct from Dönitz's HQ.

Left: General Dwight D. Eisenhower together with some of the senior American generals who helped pave the way to victory in Europe, gather at 12th Army Group HQ, Bad Wildungen, Germany, on 12 May 1945. Seated on the front row from L to R are: Lt Gen William H. Simpson (CG US Ninth Army), Gen George S. Patton, Jr, (CG US Third Army), Gen Carl A. Spaatz (CG USATAF), Gen Eisenhower, Gen Omar N. Bradley (CG 12th AG), Gen Courtney H. Hodges (CG US First Army), Lt Gen Leonard T. Gerow (CG US Fifteenth Army). (US Army)

Upper right: The Führer's mountain-top hideaway. This photograph of the 'Eagle's Lair' at Berchtesgarten was taken on 19 May 1945 and shows soldiers of the US 101st Airborne Division – appropriately nicknamed 'The Screaming Eagles' because of their shoulder insignia – lounging on the patio! (US Army via Real War Photos - A 377B)

Right: Although the top of Adolf Hitler's mountain hideaway looked fine, the lower part was gutted by fire – started by SS troops who had been left behind to guard it. (US Army via Real War Photos - A 2498)

Left: President Harry S. Truman, visiting Brussels on 15 July 1945, pauses to speak to one of the Honor Guard, furnished by 137th Inf Regt, US 35th Inf Div. (US Army via Real War Photos - A 3150)

Victory Parades

While the Western Allied Armies had halted as agreed, well to the west of Berlin, the city would be divided into zones so that all the victorious nations could be represented there. And of course it was the obvious place in which to hold Victory Parades. As the photographs show, both the Americans and British held Victory Parades in Berlin during July 1945, and in September 1945 there was another grand parade which included representatives of the Soviet Union. The 'Road to Berlin' had at long last been completed.

Right: 51st Highland Division hold a Victory Parade in Bremerhaven, 12 May 1945, at which the salute was taken by XXX Corps commander Gen Sir Brian Horrocks. Here troops of the Black Watch march past. (IWM - BU 6109)

Lower right: US Third Army review in Berlin, 20 July 1945. In the leading half-track are the US Secretary of State for War, Henry L. Stimson and Gen George S. Patton, Jr, as they drive past the tanks of US 2nd Armd Div. (US Army)

Opposite page, top: Field Marshal Montgomery, accompanied by Lt Col Pat Hobart CO 1 RTR, inspecting 1st Royal Tank Regiment in Berlin in September 1945. (Tank Museum)

Opposite page, bottom: Allied Victory Parade, 7 September 1945. A trio of Red Army JS 3 heavy tanks motor past the saluting base. Over 4,000 infantrymen and 200 AFVs, representing USA, USSR, Great Britain and France, paraded in the Tiergarten, whilst Zhukov and Patton took the salute. (IWM - AP 281590)

Bibliography

Brett-Smith, Richard. *Hitler's Generals*. Osprey, 1976

Eisenhower, General Dwight D. *Crusade in Europe*. William Heinemann Ltd, 1948

Forty, George. *The Armies of George S. Patton*. Arms and Armour Press Ltd., 1996

Joslen, Lieutenant-Colonel H. F. *Orders of Battle Second World War 1939–1945*, vol. II, HMSO, 1960

Montgomery, Field Marshal B. *Normandy to the Baltic*. Barrie & Jenkins Ltd., 1971 (in a combined volume with *El Alamein to the River Sangro*)

Toland, John. *Adolf Hitler*. Doubleday & Co. Inc., 1976

Below: Allied flag-raising ceremony in Berlin, Monday, 20 August 1945. The four principals at the ceremony were L to R: Montgomery, Zhukov, Eisenhower and Koenig. Behind them is the courthouse building where the Allied Control Council will meet to decide on policies to govern postwar Germany. (IWM - KY 495409)